Learn for Life

New Architecture for New Learning

gestalten

Intro-duction

In an era of increasing openness, transparency, and interconnectivity, strengthening and developing our institutions to accrue and share knowledge is more important than ever. The concepts and tools needed to excel and keep pace within our rapidly evolving global forum require new and diverse approaches to lifelong learning. As the realms of work, play, and formal and informal education begin to link and mix, changing attitudes in both the philosophical and architectural approaches to these spaces result in an exciting and extensive rethinking of our learning environments.

Every space can be a learning space. Whether we find ourselves in a classroom, laboratory, playground, art installation, or corporate headquarters, the architecture that surrounds us plays a crucial role in maintaining our sense of wonder and curiosity long after childhood. Through the entire developmental process, which begins with free play, continues in early to advanced school settings, and culminates in the building of career paths, work environments, civic engagement, and public forums, a person's role as a lifelong learner need never stop if nurtured effectively. By applying enthusiasm and curiosity as fundamental design concepts, these revolutionary projects help transform and reenergize how we learn and where we learn it. By revamping what learning can look like and arguing for the incorporation of fun and active engagement within the learning environment, the projects that follow actively reject insular educational models that can become limiting, both spatially and developmentally.

LIFE

Different educational experiences require a range of spaces that encourage learning and set a creative and inquisitive mood for students of every age and in any institution. The first entry point into the world of lifelong learning begins in the playground. These informal and highly adaptable spaces maintain a level of social, spatial, and programmatic openness that allow childrens' curiosity and beginners' wonder to flow unabated. Upon entering the school system, environments that cultivate a sense of fun and excitement, while also introducing more focused and independent study, become the primary influence on the programmatic layout. Serving as more focused continuations of what one learns in elementary and high school, universities and libraries offer additional inspired backdrops for information gathering, further topic development, and advanced research. Workplaces, think tanks, offices, and breakout spaces all help extend the imagination into one's professional life, establishing long-lasting forums for generating ideas, innovations, and collaborative breakthroughs.

Similar to the sequential progression of one's initial development, the first section of *Learn for Life* covers educational environments from kindergarten through university. In the wake of a growing realization that our classrooms can teach us as our teachers do, the long history of associating education with traditional, and often banal, building typologies has led to a considerable delay in the inclusion of architecture as an integral aspect of an effective and inspiring learning space. Dating back to the beginning of the Industrial Revolution, how society thinks about education began to shift to accommodate different teaching methods that focus on collaborative and progressive learning. Diverging from prior models of authoritarian teaching, where knowledge was seen as a strict and linear path between point A and point B, these new methods connected learning with flexibility and imagination. Not only did these schools make life more pleasant and interesting for the children, but as a result of their more individually responsive curriculum, such programs also produced a more creative, sociable, enterprising, and adaptive student body. While alternative approaches ranging from Montessori to Waldorf to Schools Without Borders began to appear, the spaces where these revolutionary philosophies of communal and specialized education emerged seldom reflected their inspiring ideologies. Only in the past 10 years has the educational field begun to experience noticeable advances in the architectural reshaping of its kindergartens, schools, and university spaces.

The exceptional work of Baupiloten, a Berlin-based architecture firm, serves as one of the first revolutionary examples of a complete architectural rethinking of early learning spaces. By treating kids as clients and collaborating with them to develop an overarching design strategy, the resulting architectural interventions to the Erika Mann Elementary School capture and build upon the essence of childhood imagination. The whimsical, colorful, and customizable spaces of these schools not only allow students to have more fun but also produce noticeable improvements in subject retention and performance. In this educational model, the more the student's imagination is challenged, the better the grades they get, and the more invested they become in the learning process. These dramatic redesigns of schools and kindergartens, and the impressive academic results they produce, influence everything from universities to the workplace.

The fundamental improvements made to the aesthetics of kindergarten and school design employ careful application of color, light, sense of scale, interconnectivity, and even the element of surprise, to produce a wealth of dynamic spaces for children of all age groups. By understanding the ability of architecture to shape one's development, particularly in these formative childhood years, these learning environments can now be tailored with as much precision as their curriculums. The Kekec Kindergarten by Arhitektura Jure Kotnik serves as an ideal example of this application of customizable educational spaces. The clever incorporation of multicolor rotating window screens impacts both the nature of light entering the interior and the aesthetic of the school from the exterior, while allowing the children to literally influence the way their world looks though a twist of a panel. Whether building confidence or stimulating relaxation in toddlers with lush colors and intimate hideouts, or encouraging collaboration and individual thinking in adolescents through

LONG

multipurpose areas and flexible furniture, changing our architectural approach to education allows the seed of lifelong creativity to be planted and nurtured as early as possible.

The architectural renaissance experienced in educational spaces from kindergarten through high school continues into university with the introduction of unique learning environments to foster specialized study programs. While early school settings reflect a sense of openness in regards to the variety of subjects one can study at a given time, universities differ from this model by focusing on just one or two topics. This process of narrowing the focus of learning to allow for more in-depth mastery of a particular subject creates a need for more programmatically specific spaces exemplified in João Luís Carrilho da Graça's understated, yet exceptionally elegant, music school in Lisbon, comprised of rows of unique and private practice rooms.

As university spaces may prove slightly less saturated in terms of color and graphic quality, they elicit a similar passion and sensibility towards developing one's mind and craft. Dominique Perrault's striking Woman's University in the center of Seoul provides an impressive campus model that intertwines student life with city life. By incorporating an expansive promenade through the middle axis of the site, the design effectively and unapologetically pulls the city right into the heart of the university. Offering diverse spaces to research and practice individually and collectively, the new look of the university combines a light-hearted elegance with a lively focus on play and integration within the surrounding community. The university's connection with the greater community plays a significant, and at times underestimated, role in the creation of opportunities, social change, and innovation. This advanced learning environment also doubles as a safe and public gathering space, facilitating mutual respect and providing an arena to overcome race, gender, and socio-economic marginalization.

LEARNING

Again mirroring the organic trajectory of a lifelong education, the second section of *Learn for Life* comes without a strict, predefined order. Upon completing university, what one chooses to do next is no longer fixed. What tools can be further developed and how one lives in, contributes to, and navigates through the greater society remains entirely open. Whether one explores a new subject during a weekend afternoon, visits a museum, or joins an extracurricular class, the structure and rhythm of learning can look very different while still keeping the fundamental elements of learning the same. While some may find themselves following a competitive work track immediately, others may explore the possibilities offered within libraries, community centers, and outdoor public spaces. Additionally, after retirement, people are able to once again explore the public realm, underscoring the flexibility and potential for continued learning after school.

As the look of traditional learning continues to undergo a dramatic aesthetic transformation, the appearance and architectural approach to workspaces, libraries, and other public learning settings have undergone extensive overhauls as well. Differing slightly from the order of the book by moving from the specific to the more open, the primary typologies of learning expanded on here explore the evolving attitudes towards the design of the work environment, the library, and the more unscripted places for continuing lifelong learning that include community centers, playgrounds, and even installations. Grouping these diverse typologies together allows for the introduction of educational and inspirational spaces as well as new approaches to formal and informal learning. Each category stands as a unique architectural stepping stone and incubator for education throughout one's maturation process.

The library represents another more fluid model of a learning and working space also experiencing a conceptual and physical renovation. In the wake of the digitization of most archives, periodicals, and an ever-increasing number of books, the role of the library is in the midst of a rapid evolution from a quiet and stiff reading and reference space to lively community learning hub. As the function of the library becomes less about the physicality of archival spaces and endless bookshelves and more about gathering and interacting, the shape of its architecture is opening up to new interpretations. Antje Heuer, Stefan Rettich, and Bert Hafermalz's Open-Air-Library presents an unusual and progressive model for how a library can look and function. Initiated and maintained completely by local residents, this outdoor space for book sharing remains open 24 hours a day. Linie Zweii Robi Mobile Library serves as another impressive interpretation of a contemporary library design. This library on wheels caters to underserved areas of rural Germany and offers cozy reading corners, quirky, irregular bookshelves, and large windows to entice the passersby. The reinvention of the role of the classical library as learning space now focuses as much on educating as it does on community building.

The workplace represents perhaps the most noticeable and anticipated element of post-academic learning to undergo a similarly extensive design transformation. With the era of homogenous cubicle offices coming to an end and a movement of influential start-up companies taking their place, employers are at last discovering the benefits of keeping their workers constantly inspired and playful. As the worlds of work and play begin to merge, the creative output and breakthroughs that an engaged and excited workforce are capable of increase exponentially. By investing in spaces that encourage learning as much as collaboration, relaxation, innovation, and fun, employers quickly reap the benefit of developing work environments, headquarters, think tanks, breakout spaces, and laboratories that foster a model of playful pragmatism.

Approaching the workspace as yet another opportunity to continue the learning process requires the design of these offices, headquarters, and laboratories to instill a sense of wonder, interest, and passion in its employees. The exceptionally whimsical Nestlé Innovation Lab by Rojkind Arquitectos offers its scientists not only a state-of-the-art facility to practice in but also a sculpturally provocative and bright laboratory with lounge spaces that enjoy views to the outdoors. Hassell's dtac House serves as another ideal example of how the workplace can invigorate its employees both mentally and physically. Understanding the value of investing in the health and well-being of its employees, this Bangkok headquarters embeds a variety of relaxation and study spaces, as well as a full-size running track, into the general working layout. By maintaining clear aims and goals while offering design that nurtures and motivates employees to continue learning and exploring within their field, this movement of workplace architecture boosts innovation, progress, and morale simultaneously.

Following this movement of community building, the remaining spaces touched on here explore the educational potential of playgrounds, community and cultural centers, and art installations. These unscripted public spaces produce exciting potential to extend the learning environment and its connected sense of wonder to almost any setting. The Bamboo Community Project by PT Bamboo Pure provides the local indigenous community with critical training in sustainable architectural practices in a series of entirely locally built and sourced bamboo structures. Doubling as both a training center and bridge spanning a river valley, this dramatic and impressive project allows the design of its facilities to inform and encourage both the flexible teaching and learning process of its users.

Learn for Life showcases a collection of the most recent examples of inspiring educational architecture from all corners of the world and all socioeconomic levels. This book highlights projects from both industrialized and rural communities that cater to everyone from infants to senior citizens. As people continue to live longer and become more educated, an emphasis on lifelong learning means that one's educational development doesn't just stop after high school or university but now continues through the workplace and beyond. By making learning a career rather than a requirement, creative and collaborative teaching strategies are finally replacing the era of memorization and standardized testing. *Learn for Life* presents approximately 150 projects driving this extensive global movement towards humanizing educational environments and establishing an experiential sense of place as a crucial part of the learning process.

In spite of the rapid adoption of new technologies by more economically advanced countries, these projects instead demonstrate innovative ways of gathering in spaces that defy limitations posed by class distinctions and access to resources. These educational spaces rely less on the development of so-called "smart classrooms" and technological breakthroughs and more on the nurturing of community. The trend away from the excessive application of computers and virtual learning represents an exciting and refreshing global phenomenon. From the communal bathhouse covered in chalkboards by BaO Architects in a remote area of China to BIG's youth center located in an industrialized part of Copenhagen, each project references the importance of privileging the social nuances that foster independent and inventive thinking.

All projects featured in *Learn for Life* stimulate the imagination by encouraging different modalities of learning. The facilitation of diverse learning styles that integrate spaces for introverted and extroverted educational activities creates a fluidity within the architecture that allows for multiple levels of use and meaning. The cultivation of innovative spaces in tandem with new approaches to curricula enables a long-overdue architecture revolution to occur within the educational realm.

By emphasizing projects that inspire innovation and imagination over mere execution and passive learning, *Learn for Life* argues for the importance of viewing education as a total body experience and collaborative process that continues over time. These examples challenge the mind not just with pens and paper and individual cookie-cutter desks but instead with an overarching architectural approach that can engage both the senses and the intellect simultaneously. As learning continues to spread outside of conventional classroom walls and into the city and surrounding communities, broader definitions of what an educational space can and should look like continue to evolve and influence related building typologies. As the playful nature developed within schools directly impacts the reimagining of our work spaces, so too can our think tanks and laboratories inspire the next generation of imaginative learning. Through the juxtaposition of projects such as Rudanko & Kankkunen's brightly colored and organic training center in Cambodia to SANAA's undulating, state-of-the-art learning facility in Switzerland, the architectural advancements in educational spaces remind us of the universal and undeniably human need for meaningful design to trigger and encourage the imagination at any age.

SPACES

Learning requires a sense of wonder and childlike enthusiasm that extends throughout our lives. As learning never stops, new parameters are required for conceptualizing and executing educational spaces. With the effects of one's surroundings becoming increasingly connected to one's ability to excel in both academic, professional, and social settings, the need for spaces that truly inspire and provoke a sense of curiosity in both the mind and body continues to grow. While the focus on education has been on what we need to teach and know, *Learn for Life* reframes this approach by suggesting what spaces can make this possible.

I.

First Steps First

Kindergarden

With fresh eyes, students set off into the world of learning with little more than imagination and a sense of fun to guide the way. Standing at the forefront of new architectural approaches driving the design of early learning facilities, a range of progressive approaches for welcoming students into the initial phase of learning are developing. By offering spaces that facilitate free play, individual exploration, and communal activities, these projects ensure that the first experience of the world of lifelong education is as exciting and engaging as possible. Through the whimsical use of color, intimate spatial layouts, and ample access to light and outdoor areas, these projects offer a sense of wonder and curiosity essential for a fulfilling educational experience.

Tham & Videgård Arkitekter
Tellus Nursery School

Stockholm, Sweden, *2010*

Bordering a former industrial development and a small forest, this nursery school acts as a mediator between different contexts and scales. An semi-enclosed entrance courtyard functions as a transitional exterior space for parents to meet and drop off their children. The organic layout and curved form encourages constant movement by creating a continuous space that offers exterior and interior rooms of dynamic shapes and colors. Windows are freely placed at different levels and allow for the adjustment of light and views based on the height of the children. A large main area serves as the focal point for the school, providing students of every age group space to interact, play, and work on shared activities. Individual working spaces and secluded group rooms for nap time and quiet activities complement this main space while the façade, made of 50 × 50 mm wooden panks, filters direct sunlight into the interior.

Rosan Bosch & Rune Fjord
Ordrup School

Gentofe, Denmark, *2006*

The design of Ordrup school contrasts with the traditional design of school interiors and instead develops hybrid spaces that double as active educational tools for differentiated teaching and creative thinking. As all children learn and think differently, the overall design encourages flexibility and collaboration, while maintaining specific areas tailored to the needs of each age group. The separation of activities creates an optimized space for diversity in both teaching and play. In the younger classes, the concepts of peace and absorption are emphasized in a series of upholstered reading tubes, while movable rugs create temporary spaces for discussion and cooperation. Students in mid-range age levels work together in smaller forums inside bright, sculptural elements or withdraw to the colorful concentration booths for reading and other work activities. The oldest classes connect teenagers to the real world and use moveable sofa islands for concentrated group work, loud discussions, and movie showings.

Elap Arquitectos

Nursery 8 units

Velez-Rubio, Spain, *2009*

Designed for children up to three years of age, fun and color represent the central themes driving this project. Distinct classrooms offer the children exposure to different colors based on their age and developmental needs: blue to promote relaxation in one-year-olds, orange to stimulate two-year-olds, and green to encourage contact with nature in three-year-olds. Common spaces surround a central playground and use mixed colors to encourage socialization and community. The smooth circle pattern punctuating the façade allows for multiple uses, for example as table, seat, and hammock, while also encouraging the children to explore and engage with their surroundings.

Alejandro Muñoz Miranda
Educational Center

Granada, Spain, *2010*

This educational center derives its design from a process of compressing and decompressing the building's massing to accommodate a range of programmatic needs. The sections of the floor plan fluctuate depending on use, e.g. smaller, lower spaces for bathrooms and larger, taller spaces for classrooms. The upper corners of the taller spaces allow for colorful skylights to be inserted, illuminating the rooms and playfully breaking up the monolithic, white exterior. Classrooms connected by a glowing corridor extend around a central, outdoor covered playground, which helps link and unify the building with both the outdoors and other interior spaces.

Magén Arquitectos
Kindergarten Rosales del Canal

Zaragoza, Spain, *2009*

Focusing on a child's unique perception of the constructed environment, this modular kindergarten combines sensitivity to scale with a strong sensorial connection to its architecture. Classrooms are organized around a central courtyard and achieve a constant connection to the outdoors through the abundant use of windows and skylights. The combination of horizontal and vertical wooden panels and colored boards extending throughout the school creates an adventurous composition that introduces a playful air into an otherwise strict, linear façade.

Sau Taller d'Arquitectura
& Lluís Jordà Sala
La Cabanya Nursery Torelló

Barcelona, Spain, *2010*

Surrounded by an urban park, this nursery school enjoys ample views of the outdoors. Laid out in three intertwined parts, the design includes space for classrooms, management, services, and a central multipurpose area that acts as a cafeteria, winter courtyard, and performance hall. Clean lines, bright colors, natural daylight, and exposure to the community all work together to provide students with an uplifting learning space and a strong sense of community.

Arhitektura Jure Kotnik
Kekec Kindergarten

Ljubljana, Slovenia, *2010*

An addition to an existing kindergarten, the redesign of Kebec Kindergarten rectifies the original school's noticeable lack of play equipment. The new rotating façade doubles as both a sunshade and an element for playing and learning that spans along the three exterior walls. These revolving slats are painted a natural wood color on one side, and nine bright colors on the other, providing children with exposure to a variety of color combinations. At times understated, and at other moments a dazzling rainbow, this unusual kindergarten offers children the rare chance to have the way they play and learn directly influence and change the appearance of their surroundings.

Van Rooijen Nourbakhsh Architecten

De Ridderhof – After School Day Care

Utrecht, Netherlands, *2007*

This project functions as a multipurpose, after-school day care and as an extension to an existing school. The spaces serve the school during daytime hours and the day-care center after school hours. In order to successfully fulfill both functions, there is custom-designed, flexible furniture, including movable tables and shelves that open and close based on the needs of the kids before, during, and after school. The use of cheerful colors and meticulously detailed furnishings create a cheerful environment, while allowing the same spaces to have multiple uses.

Van Rooijen Nourbakhsh Architecten
Playground Building

Utrecht, Netherlands, *2010*

Accessible to children from the surrounding neighborhoods, this playground building functions as a modest and durable safe haven that appeals to both kids and their parents. The building includes a play area and separate spaces for a kindergarten. By means of a movable partition, these spaces can be interlinked to provide room for different activities and multiple uses. Natural wood and bright colors establish a cozy and comfortable atmosphere in the interior spaces. This colorful, light-hearted project connects inside and outside, providing large openings and windows to the exterior and a covered canopy for outdoor play.

studiomas architetti associati
Nursery School in Fossalunga

Fossalunga di Vedelago, Italy, *2009*

Situated on the outskirts of a small village near Venice, this school serves as an educational transition space between town and nature. Intersected by a bright circulation passage, the school is organized around a central hall with classrooms extending from it. Circulation corridors vary in dimension, color, and function, creating a range of proportions and atmospheres based on the function of each space.

Karl-Heinz Winkens & Marcel Klebs

Forscherkindergarten

Berlin, Germany, *2011*

Situated atop a small hill surrounded by trees, this single-story kindergarten offers a centrally located and open communal space along a row of secondary rooms and a garden. The arrangement of the classrooms and the multipurpose area underlines the linearity of the building while providing a direct connection to the outdoors. The kindergarden enjoys a terrace located at the end of the building which opens out into the garden and connects the rooms to the outside. Natural materials add to the building's aesthetic and a green roof provides solar energy for the school.

Petersen Pörksen Partner Architekten & Stadtplaner
Lübeck Kindergarten of Music and Art

Lübeck, Germany, *2011*

This three-story brick building integrates into the site by establishing strong visual connections between interior and exterior. Large apertures extend out through the façade, creating visual intrigue for the surrounding city and useful play areas and lookout points for the children inside.

Feld72

Kindergarten Terenten

Terenten, Italy, *2010*

Located in South Tyrol, a border region where German, Italian, and Ladin cultures overlap, this kindergarten mediates and transcends its influential neighbors. The school emerges from the foot of the Alps, integrating one face into the landscape and becoming an independent building on the other. The project relates to the scale of the surrounding village and also integrates the perspective of the children into the design concept. The kindergarten combines the elemental logic of the overall form with a complexity of its inner and outer spatial sequences, providing a number of nooks and intimate spaces for the children to explore. Using traditional and contextual architectural elements and simultaneously translating them into a contemporary form creates both a dynamic architectural vernacular and an exciting educational space.

Archivision Hirotani Studio
Hirotani Yoshihiro
& Ishida Yusaku

Leimond-Nagahama Nursery School

Nagahama, Japan, *2011*

Located on the outskirts of Nagahama, this nursery school serves children from zero to five years old. Planned as a single-story structure, the project provides a feeling of transparency between its interior spaces and the exterior landscape. Conical, square light wells of varying shapes, colors, and directionalities create lofty ceilings for the spaces and allow unique and ever-changing light patterns to illuminate the main nursery area. This house of light presents children with a personalized and ongoing invitation to chase, play, and study the rays as they traverse the space throughout the day.

Die Baupiloten

Kindergarten Taka-Tuka-Land

Berlin, Germany, *2007*

Named after a fictional island in the South Seas, this kindergarten is situated in an oasis of greenery. An architectural interpretation of a children's story in which the main character lives inside an old oak tree and makes lemonade, this intriguing school erases distinctions between indoors and outdoors, and spaces for playing and working. The bright yellow interior breaches the exterior walls, resulting in a dynamic, sheltered, and padded structure to climb, hide, and nap on in any weather. Within the interior spaces, children can immerse themselves in a colorful land filled with personal nooks and play areas in varying heights and sizes.

Catherine Cheung
Starlit Learning Centre

Hong Kong, China, *2010*

This whimsical center provides performance training for toddlers from two- to six-years-old. In contrast to the high-pressure study environments most Hong Kong children are subjected to, this project offers a delightful and relaxing learning atmosphere for studying. Located in a relatively narrow building with an oversized, one-meter column cutting through it, this multipurpose center carefully maximizes its limited space. By integrating this design obstacle instead of working around it, the project forges a new a link between classrooms and a zone for other activities. Inspired by the scenery of New York's Central Park, the interior walls overflow with a variety of materials, patterns, and colors to reflect a sense of connection to nature and general tranquility. Secret spaces and hidden attics appear in the space, catering to a child's love for adventure and exploration.

Henning Larsen Architects
Elverhøj Day Care Center

Holbæk, Denmark, *2009*

Designed to promote feelings of community and spaciousness, this day care accommodates 136 children ranging in age from zero to six years old. Wedged into the site's dominant hillside, the building boasts a large green roof and offers a seamless transition between architecture and landscape. The energy-efficient green roof naturally cools the building during the summer and provides heat insulation throughout the winter. The center of the project uses tall glass windows to direct daylight far into the building. Organized into two wings, the nursery occupies the first, while older children are located in the second. A plant and herb bed for the children and large flowerpots for the nursery offer shade from the sun, while also creating a climatic buffer from the cold, allowing children to play outside without wearing gloves. The walking areas of the center form an additional climate zone that shields against direct sunlight and prevents overheating of the playrooms. These walking areas are heated in the spring and fall, making it possible to also use them as additional play areas.

Tezuka Architects
Ring Around a Tree

Tokyo, Japan, *2011*

Inspired by the vice principal of the school's request to have "a classroom without furniture," this annex to Fuji Kindergarten contains English classrooms and a school-bus waiting area that blur borders between interior and exterior and bases the general scale and circulation of the spaces on the needs and interests of the children rather than the adults. With many ceiling heights being just tall enough for a child to pass through and platforms located at varying climbing levels, the design of this school puts the experience of the child at the forefront, encouraging curiosity, bravery, and mastering one's surroundings. Built around a twisting old zelkova tree, existing branches penetrate the building, creating a dynamic and evolving relationship as the tree grows over time.

Fuji

Tezuka Architects
Takaharu & Yui Tezuka
Fuji Kindergarten
Tokyo, Japan, *2007*

Constructed around three large zelkova trees, Fuji Kindergarten functions as a building without walls and without dead ends. Rejecting traditional spatial hierarchies and the inevitable segregation that comes with them, this school equalizes both the students and the faculty in a single continuous open space, improving tendencies towards bullying and isolation. Piles of wooden blocks and casually placed furniture stand as the sole partitions between different class areas. Obscuring the distinction between traditional school and outdoor corridor, this kindergarten building remains entirely open to the outdoors for more than 8 months a year.

Mum is shocked
Because they look smart
Dad is feeling happy
12th
November
Friday
put your hand up
ssssss
mmmooo

II.

Trial and Error

School

Finding one's way and strengthening character and identity during school often proves to be the most challenging phase of lifelong learning. As children advance into elementary school and then into high school, their learning spaces promote independence and more structured courses of study. Choreographing spaces that enable topic finding and building results in a series of flexible and multipurpose areas that allow students to experiment and engage with their surroundings. These mixed-use programmatic layouts encourage students to gather, work, and play together or separately depending on the task at hand. By mixing elements of more formal design restraint with areas that inspire participation and group play, these schools instill students with a feeling of academic responsibility embedded within an overarching structure of fun and self awareness.

3XN

Ørestad Gymnasium

Copenhagen, Denmark, 2007

Ørestad Gymnasium stands as the first high school in Denmark based upon the new reforms of the Danish educational systems for students from 16 to 19 years old. The key principals of both this reform and this project encourage communication and interaction while striving to achieve a more life-like studying environment. Interconnected vertically and horizontally, four study zones occupy each floor of the four-story building. Avoiding level changes maximizes the organizational flexibility and enables the different teaching and learning spaces to overlap and interact with no distinct borders. The rotation of each floor plate opens a part of every floor to the vertical central atrium, forming a zone that provides a space for community and expresses the school's ambition to provide interdisciplinary education.

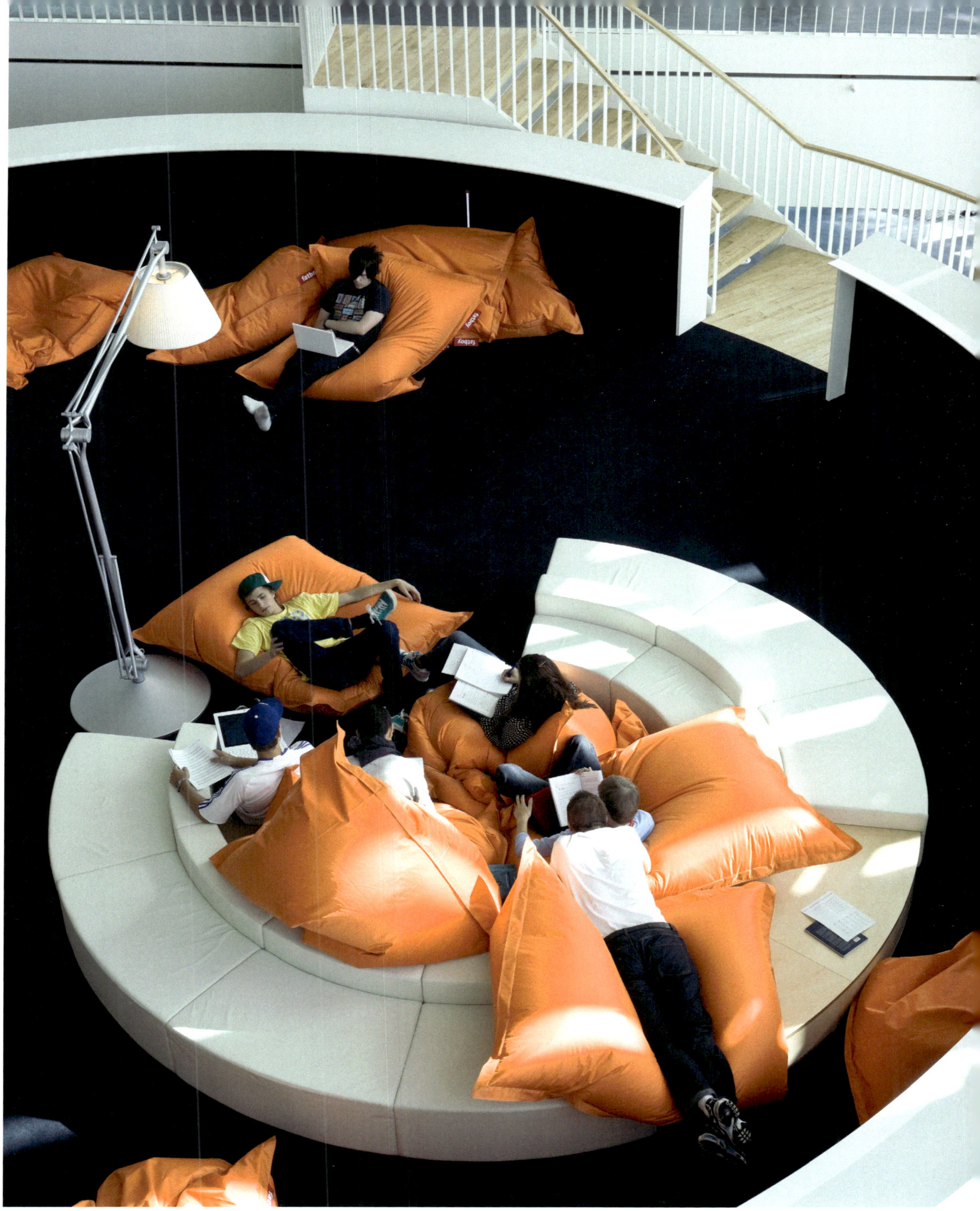

Sako Architects
Zigzag

Tianjin, China, *2011*

Comprising a middle and elementary school, library, gymnasium, and dining hall, this highly geometric and futuristic design provides a series of light-filled and colorful spaces for learning and exploration. A large roof filled with round skylights connects the spaces between schoolhouses and creates a fantastically surreal semi-outdoor public space perfect for play, socializing, and performance. 12 pastel colored bridges connect the classroom buildings and provide a constant and otherworldly vitality to the space as children move across them.

i29

School 01

Amsterdam, Netherlands, *2005*

Located within the Caland Lyceum's new building designed by Bos&Partners Architects, the goal of this interior design intervention is to create a distinctive, playful, and unique identity for the school, while capturing the student body's passion for sports. This project encompasses the main hall, staff room, library, and media room and covers each space and its furniture in bright, graphic, sports-related colors. The incorporation of multipurpose and mobile furniture becomes a central element in the project's design strategy, as benches and tables of varying heights allow students to sit, lie, hang, lean, or relocate them. These interior installations actively contrast with the building's anonymous grey brick and glass wall exterior, injecting the interior spaces with a sense of fun and vibrancy.

Die Baupiloten

Carl Bolle Elementary School

Berlin, Germany, *2008*

Located in the urban district of Berlin-Moabit, the development of language skills and physical activity serve as the main focus at this sports-oriented school. Updating the existing school to make it a full-time educational space, this project transforms the original ground floor into a playful leisure area. Based loosely upon a children's spy story, the development of various spaces promote communication, movement, and investigation. The multipurpose layout provides the children with listening areas, reading retreats, and climbing walls which lead to elevated observation posts. These spaces also allow the children to explore scientific phenomena in a youthful and energetic environment.

Die Baupiloten
Erika Mann Elementary School II

Berlin, Germany, *2008*

This whimsical school provides unique and lively interior spaces where children can immerse themselves in a colorful land, filled with personal nooks and play areas in varying heights and sizes. In these hideouts, children create their own environment through the manipulation of sound, light, and image. A relaxation room, located on the third floor, offers a landscape of seating-pedestals covered with foam, tarp, and textiles. A series of one-meter high "petals" form a protective island around the pedestals, large enough for two to three children. These protective islands are made of wooden frames and can be individually constructed by the children, enabling them to directly influence and shape their environment.

Carrilho da Graça arquitectos
João Luís Carrilho da Graça

Renovation and Extension of the German School of Lisbon

Lisbon, Portugal, *2010*

This extension to an existing German school consists of a new elementary school and gymnasium. Built on the southern side of the site, the volume of the elementary school extends over two levels and is partially buried. The school extension defines the spatial limits of the project and operates as an acoustic barrier that buffers noise from the neighboring highway. On the northern side, the pure volume of the gymnasium blends with the existing auditorium building, redrawing and energizing the school's entrance square.

DEUTSCHE SCHULE

Allied Works – Brad Cloepfil
Booker T. Washington High School for the Performing and Visual Arts

Dallas, Texas, USA, *2008*

A renovation and expansion of a historic 1922 building, this project includes new classrooms and studios for the core programs of music, dance, theater, and visual arts, as well as spaces for assembly, performance, and traditional academic instruction. The expansion provides simple loft spaces that orient around and extend outward from an open-air, central amphitheater. The different programs produce individual identities and dedicated resources while still overlapping with adjacent disciplines in plan and section. Two four-story atriums are situtated between the main program areas and facilitate open circulation, light, and views, while covered outdoor areas encourage interaction and protect from the elements.

EXIT

Sarah Wigglesworth Architects

Sandal Magna Primary School

Wakefield, UK, *2010*

Designed as a flagship eco-school, this building stands as one of the most carbon efficient schools in the UK. Accommodating 210 pupils between the ages of five and eleven and a nursery, the school also contains a community room for parents for adult education and group activities. The school's design takes its cue from its vernacular surroundings, referencing the pattern of terraced houses and back streets with three parallel, single-story wings made from local reclaimed red brick. A range of cladding materials including raw timber, weatherboarding, and corrugated rain screens denote different uses within the school and add further interest to the angular geometries of the building. Flexible classroom design and a street-like layout encourage interaction between students of different age groups. The layout avoids hidden corners and blind spots. Careful landscaping provides different types of outdoor play space including areas for learning, planting, quiet zones, and games. Each classroom offers direct access to the outdoor playgrounds and views to the surrounding landscape.

Huma Arquitectura

Nursery – Elementary School

Roldán, Spain, *2010*

Wrapped in a green carpet of artificial turf, this unusual school of staggered angles fluctuates between meeting conventional expectations of a learning facility and complete surrealism. The incorporation of a number of linear elements and a relatively typical courtyard design juxtapose with the roofline's steep angles and the unexpected texture and color covering every exterior surface. With no material distinction made between walls and roof, the matte color of the turf collapses the project's spatiality to make the buildings read as a series of paper-thin cutouts. Such a visually charged and tactile project creates an optimal setting for inspiring and exploring.

Verstas Architects
Kirkkojärvi Comprehensive School

Espoo, Finland, *2010*

The goals for this school combine functionality, comfort, efficiency, and ecology into a unified design approach for preschoolers and children from six to sixteen years old. Common spaces and the high school form the first and larger curved mass while the smaller, intimate spaces of the elementary school comprise the other. Functioning as a small, lively city, all classes have their own home areas with dedicated lobbies, entrances, and color schemes. These home areas are separated from the more public central space while still keeping the distances in between as short as possible. The development of a close connection between classrooms and yard spaces makes going outside especially inviting for the children. School facilities double as multipurpose spaces for local residents to enjoy music and social activities during the evenings.

24h Architecture
Maartje Lammers, Boris Zeisser, Olav Bruin & Andrew Duff
Panyaden School
Chiang Mai, Thailand, *2011*

Situated in the lush green surroundings of a former fruit orchard, this 5,000-square-meter bilingual elementary school consists of an informal arrangement of pavilions organized along pathways inspired by the shape of the tropical antler horn fern. Load-bearing walls made from rammed earth form the partitions for the classroom pavilions while the outer walls are constructed from adobe. A combination of glass windows framed by recycled local hardwood, bottles, and washing machine windows all bring natural light into the classrooms. Cupboards, shelves, and secret play areas are built into the surrounding adobe walls. The curved contours of the bamboo roof structure evoke the impressive formations of the mountains surrounding the site. A larger pavilion, supported by bamboo bundled columns functions as the assembly hall and canteen, and elicits a feeling of walking though a dense bamboo forest. Panyaden School delivers a holistic education that integrates Buddhist principles and environmental awareness in an architecturally dynamic and ecological space.

Song:
Good,
and, You
your hand, You
and,

Anna Heringer & Eike Roswag
School Handmade in Bangladesh

Rudrapur, Bangladesh, *2005*

Made out of local earth and bamboo, this school promotes the individual abilities and interests of the children, offering both an alternative curriculum and a refreshing space in which to learn it. The ground floor's thick, earthen walls house three classrooms that open onto an organically shaped system of indoor caves. These cozy indoor tunnels serve as a safe haven for the children to gather. In contrast to the heavy and solid first floor, the upper level uses a bamboo structure to create an open-plan room filled with light. Shadows and sunrays stream through the bamboo strips and play across the floor, accentuating the colorful materials of the saris hung across the ceiling. An outdoor platform extends into the surrounding trees, providing a sensation of verticality and color in an environment of predominantly small, low, and monotone earthen dwellings.

G. studio Architects,
Bruno Kubler Landscape,
Hagenmuller, Jost, E3

Groupe Scolaire – Elementary and Maternal School

Willgotheim, France, *2009*

This school serves as an educational oasis in a pristine natural setting. The minimalist and understated design provides spacious classrooms brimming with natural light and inspiring scenic vistas. Flexible partitions allow for spaces to be joined together for communal activities and events, while a rustic fence encloses an outdoor garden for the children.

Frei Rezakhanlou Architects
Chermignon School, Kindergarten and Multi-purpose Hall

Chermignon, Switzerland, *2010*

Serving as the connection point between five small villages, this school complex provides a variety of outdoor spaces for children to play in, as well as crucial meeting spaces for people from the region to gather. Built on a steep site, the buildings and retaining walls are set around a central forum. The school and the hall share the same roof, which facilitates the use of the sports hall by pupils and vice-versa. The kindergarten overlooks a spectacular alpine vista across the valley and provides a direct access to the main playground.

Mcbride Charles Ryan
Penleigh and Essendon Grammar School – Junior Boys Building

Melbourne, Australia, *2011*

This unusual two-story addition to an Australian grammar school acknowledges and cultivates its unique urban condition and the transformative role architecture can play in child development. A massive, uniform façade abstracted from the silhouette of a typical federation home provides the building with a highly graphic identity. Northern courtyards extend off the ground-floor classrooms while the upstairs corridor reverts to increase a feeling of privacy. The interior spaces offer undulating and vaulted spaces, reflecting the building's irregular exterior and creating a dynamic space for learning and self-discovery.

Cottrell & Vermeulen Architecture
Krishna-Avanti Primary School

Harrow, United Kingdom, *2009*

The first voluntary-aided Hindu School in the UK, the architecture of this project reflects the Hindu community, while functioning as a state of the art educational facility and an environmentally sustainable building. Extensive community outreach establishes an ethos for the school based on Hindu beliefs. At the heart of the integrated school landscape stands the deities, Krishna and Balarama, housed in an impressive white marble temple carved in India. The deities watch over the children, and activities within their gaze focus on worship, dining, music, dance, and yoga. The classrooms each enjoy a view of the temple and open onto a vegetable garden and playground. Conceived as a series of outdoor classrooms, vegetable gardens, fruit orchards, playgrounds, and a wildlife habitat, this school seamlessly integrates into the landscape, providing a stimulating and peaceful environment for educational and spiritual development.

4
2

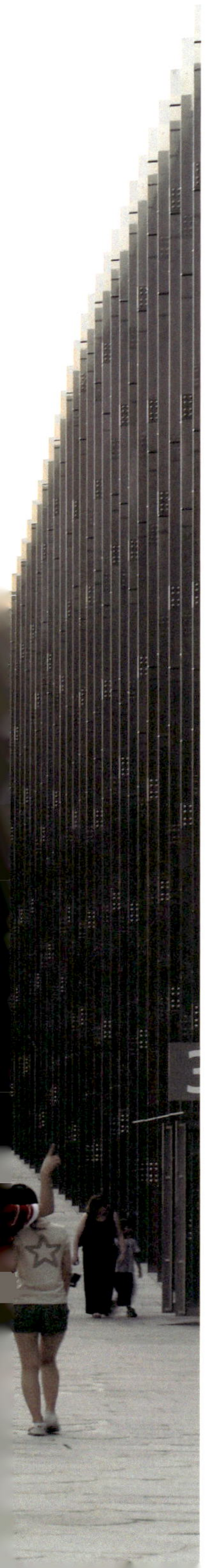

III.

On Campus

University

Additional exploration into professional topics and specializations can continue within a university setting. Now fully independent learners, university students can apply their academic tools in an environment that encourages mastery of particular crafts, and bridges the realm of school with the outside world. Universities included in this section foster both focused and social forums for continued learning by intertwining communal classrooms and social areas with individual practice rooms and study spaces. Additionally, these projects integrate the richness of the surrounding community as an essential element influencing the greater architectural layout, thereby connecting students to the world that awaits them after school.

Carrilho da Graça arquitectos
João Luís Carrilho da Graça
School of Music of the Polytechnic Institute

Lisbon, Portugal, *2008*

Conveying the conviviality and extroversion inherent in certain musical forms, this music school visually connects the interior with the exterior, while still maintaining the seclusion and soundproofing necessary for the more private and reflective practice spaces. A combination of concrete and wood provide both the soundproofing and acoustic reverberation for the different rooms. With minimal detailing on the exterior, strategically located glass panels provide intimate, yet silent, glimpses into the interior practice rooms, showcasing a dazzling variety of musical instruments and the discipline needed to master them.

Supermachine Studio

BUCC, Bangkok University Creative Center

Bangkok, Thailand, *2010*

Serving as a facility to test emerging ideas for the creative economy, this project occupies the first and second floor of Bangkok University's new building. The main workshop, clad with an ever-changing message board comprised of 10,000 pieces of custom-made, brightly colored plastic units, encourages communication and creative expression. The students can modify the wall's colors by rotating the pixel units to leave messages for their friends or simply to create new patterns or hues for the room. The theme of flexibility and adaptability also extends into the facility's office area, where staff work at a long, communal table allowing for an ongoing reshuffling of seating assignments based on changing tasks and spatial requirements.

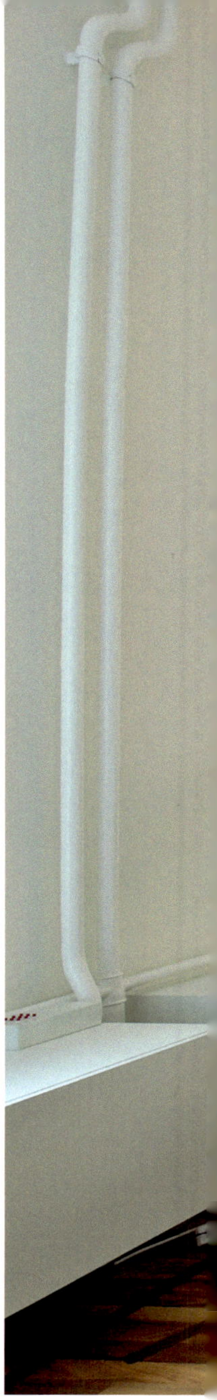

Simone Ashoff
with Jeanette Bergen & Mai-Britt Mikolajewicz
Good School

Hamburg, Germany, *2009*

Located in a former veterinary office in a bustling area of Hamburg, the Good School acts as Germany's biggest hub for the exchange of digital knowledge. Since 2009, this collective has trained more than 400 creative professionals from over 30 companies in a variety of digital tools. The Good School teacher network consists of more than 100 national and international experts who offer a diverse range of training in the fields of technology and marketing. The interior of the Good School mixes the nostalgia of old-fashioned classrooms with contemporary technology, innovative showpieces, and interactive exhibitions. From more classical lectures to live concerts, group meetings, and social media fire drills, this organization remains dedicated to the transmission of knowledge and lifelong education.

goodsummerschool.posterous.com
good2Know
goodsummerschool@posterous.com

Coop Himmelb(l)au
Wolf D. Prix & Partner

Central Los Angeles Area High School #9 for the Visual and Performing Arts

California, USA, *2008*

Part of the Los Angeles Unified School District's rigorous state bond to fund 155 new schools by 2012, this performing arts high school rests on a 9.8-acre site in the heart of downtown Los Angeles. The school accommodates 1,800 students and offers courses in the visual and performing arts, music, and dance. Fulfilling its mandate as a public facility, the school includes a professional performing arts theater for just under 1,000 visitors. The project consists of seven buildings, the theater, four classroom buildings, the library, and the cafeteria. An expressive, spiralling steel structure hovers over the campus, serving as an iconic marker for the school and the city.

SANAA
Rolex Learning Center

Lausanne, Switzerland, *2010*

Housing one the largest scientific collections in Europe, the Rolex Learning Center functions as a laboratory for learning, a library, and an international cultural hub for both students and the general public. Spread over one single fluid space of 20,000 square meters, the expansive building provides a seamless network of services, libraries, social and study spaces, restaurants, cafes, and stunning outdoor areas. The building lifts up along each edge to integrate entrances. Undulating floors and curved patios subtly divide the different programs while simultaneously connecting them, allowing for multipurpose uses and increased social interaction. Lacking traditional visual and spatial boundaries between areas, the library instead groups silent and calm zones along its interior hills and slopes. Fourteen voids of varying dimensions are cut from the structure to create round courtyards and a visual link between the interior and exterior. This highly intimate yet public space emphasizes collaborative, cross-disciplinary research and flexibility of use.

Dominique Perrault Architecture
EWHA Woman's University

Seoul, South Korea, *2008*

EHWA's campus weaves the school and the surrounding city together through the creation of a massive campus valley. A vibrant hillside with a promenade for circulation sliced through it, this project maintains a strong relationship to the outdoors, as it literally carves its interior spaces from these earthen mounds. The interior classrooms and forums open onto the central promenade, encouraging interaction with the community at large and extending the learning environment into the surrounding landscape. Oscillating between building, landscape, and sculpture, this bold formal parting of the land results in a dynamic and visually compelling experience that beckons both the students and the passerby alike to linger and explore.

9

109
109
106
106

Date Café

IV.

Knowledge Base

Library

The function of the library plays an integral role in one's learning process at any age. In spite of the evolving use of the library as it transitions into the era of online databases and archives, this learning typology remains an important space for developing knowledge and connecting with community. Accessible to all, the library represents a model of exploratory learning that can continually grow and shift over time. These compelling public learning spaces utilize color, light, and connection to both books and one another, to invigorate and instill pride in one's ongoing educational pursuits. Catering towards everyone from young to old, these libraries present new architectural typologies for connecting with the general public through a shared interest in accruing knowledge.

Rosan Bosch & Rune Fjord

Hjørring Central Library

Hjørring, Denmark, *2008*

As the role of the library continues to evolve, the design of this project focuses on the shifting relationship with the library and transforms it into a meeting place that encourages engagement, participation, and development. The heart of this new library rests in the physical communication structure that twists and winds its way through the library, breaking through walls, floors, and bookcases. Sometimes a counter and at others a shelf, the structure points, guides, and tempts the visitors to explore and interact with all parts of the library. This band doubles as both decoration and an active communication tool for the library staff. The bright bubble wall functions similarly, providing large holes for exhibiting and presenting reviews. Nurturing both a visual and emotional connection between the children's area and the general section of the library results in a pervasive overall youthful feeling and provides a fluid transition between children, youth, and adult areas. This library serves as a new platform for finding knowledge, communication, and inspiration.

Dyrenes kappestrid

Eventyr

GALAXY DNA IPOD
REVOLUTION ON OFF
SOCIETY
POLITICS
REFORM
TRAGEDY
STATISTICS
RICH
POOR
LIFE IS BEAUTIFUL
ME
WIRELESS
b
a

Projektil Architekti
National Technical Library

Prague, Czech Republic, *2009*

The NTL functions as a publicly accessible scientific and technical library. Housing the largest Czech collection of domestic and foreign documents in the fields of technology and the applied natural and social sciences, this library contains a unique collection of over 1.2 million volumes of books, magazines, newspapers, and scientific works. The impressive concrete structure hosts a central atrium full of skylights and covered in playful illustrations and bright flooring. This atrium, combined with a network of brightly lit study and lounge areas, creates the ideal atmosphere for curiosity, personalization, and comfort.

ff-Architekten
Feldhusen & Fleckenstein
with Martina Wronna
and Raum-Bewegung

Library in Luckenwalde Railway Station

Luckenwalde, Germany, *2008*

This public library is located within a building formerly used by passenger trains. The extensive renovation of both the interior and the façade was done with the local children and adolescents in mind. The result of this new building provides a sense of identity, place, and urban expression to a railway station otherwise lacking in any of the characteristics that make a space feel personal, exciting, and unique. The tilted extension to the building puts the library into a new urban context, while the shimmering, gold façade emphasizes the library's place in the community, subtly reflecting the movements of people walking by and the surrounding buildings and trees. Inside, children and adolescents each have special rooms to inspire and accommodate their different needs and interests. Brimming with historical materials, colors, and playful finishes, these spaces provide young people with creative and thoughtful spaces for exploring, thinking, and thriving.

fatboy

kwint Architects
Culture Campus Vleuterweide

Utrecht, Netherlands, *2009*

This information plaza uses large wooden benches to perform a variety of functions for this cultural gathering space. Creating a landscape comprised of solid, warm colors, the wooden planks integrate an assortment of furniture, lounge spaces, information screens, presentation columns, bulletin boards, and folder displays seamlessly into their surfaces.

Sako Architects – Keiichiro Sako, Shuhei Aoyama & Yu Fujita
Kid's Republic

Shanghai, China, 2008

Located on a bustling Shanghai avenue, this picture-book store develops a world of fantasy and imagination. Integrating the theme of trees and forest, a large tree trunk, cut and processed into many pieces, is embedded into the space forming the ceiling, walls, stairs and furniture. Floor to ceiling bookcases varying in width and depth fill the walls of the ground-floor space. The second floor houses a hemispherical activity area clad with rough bark on the exterior and painted a bright white on the interior. The ceiling of this space fills with light through a series of irregular round holes propagated across the top. Covered in a colourful plush carpet, the ground varies in height, creating a flexible stage, auditorium, and reading room.

Platvorm

Papiria

The Hague, Netherlands, *2010*

The fully refurbished Children's Book Museum invites everyone from beginning readers through seventh-grade students to explore the world of letters. The museum's exhibition, Papiria, encourages children to take on their own writing projects. Designed as a literary landscape with six different areas, Papiria introduces children to key writing elements including character development and story line. The surreal and expressive installation transports visitors away from the museum floor and into the imaginative world of the story. Children engage with the story as they collect crucial items for the plot, read, discuss, and eventually develop their own unique characters to integrate back into their surrounding literary wonderland.

Foster & Partners
Free University Library

Berlin, Germany, *2005*

This all-white futuristic library offers a dynamic space flooded with diffused light, ideal for study and research. Situated within a panellized dome varying in transparency, the interior stacks and reading areas stand autonomously from the façade, lifting off the ground and spreading over three levels. These offset, undulating floor plates hover over one another, providing personalized work stations that maintain visual connectivity between levels.

Wurm & Wurm
Architekten Ingenieure
Media Centre Oberkirch

Oberkirch, Germany , *2010*

An organically formed and centrally positioned stairwell connects the three levels of this media center. The open staircase not only serves as a dynamic movement and communication zone but also transmits light from the ceiling glazing into the space. Large apertures in the façade resemble shop-windows, presenting varied and exciting views of the surrounding town. The external, brighter, glazed areas house the reading zones and provide furniture that can transform from bench to table, which encourages users to stay and linger. This sculptural media center, creates a rich spatial experience- and communication hub for any age.

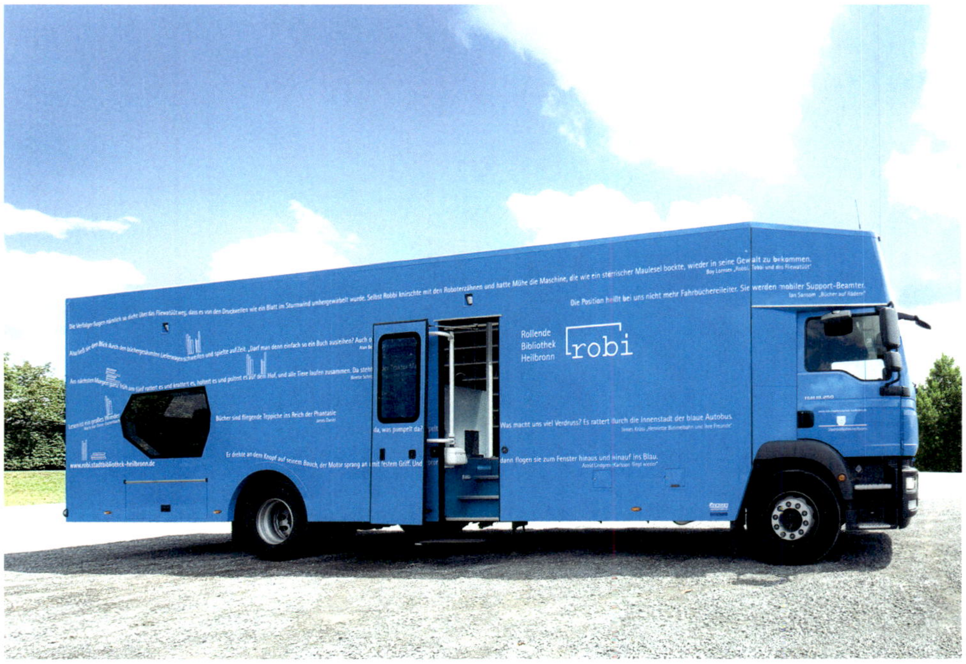

Linie Zweii

Robi Mobile Library

Heilbronn, Germany, *2011*

This library on wheels provides rural areas of Germany access to a variety of books and an impressive space in which to enjoy them. A series of undulating shelves create a playful interior atmosphere, while also extending to the exterior of the bus in the form of inspiring quotations from literature. Red cube seats integrated into the shelving can be moved freely across the space. A large window brings natural daylight into the space while offering a glimpse of the trove of books that have come to visit.

Wiel Arets Architects
University Library Utrecht UBU

Utrecht, Netherlands, *2004*

The University Library serves as an austere and elegant addition to the university complex in the city of Utrecht. The library's organization reconciles the paradoxical requirement of needing both closed spaces to store and protect books and opens spaces for studying and researching. By suspending the opaque, closed volumes overhead, the ground plane becomes free to accommodate visitors. Patterns of leaves printed onto the glazed façades connect the building to nature while also diffusing sunlight. From the main entrance, a wide staircase leads to the auditorium and exhibition space, and then continues further to the actual library area on the first level. The large lending area and central desk are situated beyond these entrance gateways in an impressive void space that extends to very top of the building.

Sou Fujimoto Architects
Musashino Art University Museum & Library

Tokyo, Japan, *2010*

Part of the expansion of a Japanese art university, this two-story library creates the feeling of being in a light-filled, infinite forest of books. The project develops this impression by wrapping the nine-meter-high walls entirely in bookshelves, punctuated by large apertures. These floor-to-ceiling bookshelves move through the space and eventually become the external walls, effectively muting the distinction between interior and exterior, and encouraging people walking by to explore the library's extensive collection.

Coelacanth K&H Architects
Kazumi Kudo & Hiroshi Horiba
Kanazawa Umimirai Library

Kanazawa, Japan, *2011*

This library consists of a single, quiet, and tranquil room filled with soft light, reading spaces, and an exposed book collection. As Japanese libraries move towards a new model that encourages readers to stay and linger, the act of creating a space that envelops the user in books strives to recapture the essence of the traditional library model while also invigorating a new sense of public values. Reflecting the general trend for libraries to facilitate reading as well as other functions, this project uses compact automated shelves that operate as a closed stack system. The facility serves as a new hub for social life, promoting exchange among the local community. Comfortable reading rooms offer visitors a pleasant, atmospheric space to read. The façade wrapping the cavernous reading room features approximately 6,000 small openings across its surface, allowing a diffused, uniform light to illuminate the space and create the optimal setting for delving into the world of human imagination.

Ricardo Bak Gordon
Garcia D' Orta Secundary School

Porto, Portugal, *2011*

This elegant addition housing a library, auditorium, and cafeteria breathes new life into the surrounding existing high school. The longitudinally placed building allows for the creation of a covered outdoor plaza that serves as a social and circulatory epicenter for the entire school. A white, austere volume with a warm, red underside provides a series of spacious and vibrant indoor and outdoor areas to cultivate creative and collaborative learning.

DAP studio
Elsa Morante Library

Lonate Ceppino, Italy, *2008*

This municipal library stands as the result of a careful restoration of and extension to the former Oratory of San Michele. The key to interpreting the project lies in the dialectic between the existing structure and the new building as it integrates tactility with lightness, opacity with refraction, and the distinctive features inherent in each volume. The white-metal library extension rises parallel to the east front of the Oratory. An enclosed box connects the two buildings, providing access to the library during the day while transforming into a lantern at night. On the ground floor, an additional box hovers in the space, creating a tunnel to link the service block with the main area lined with bookcases. This project offers a dynamic space for learning where architecture can exist and dematerialize simultaneously and boundaries between interior and exterior, old and new all but disappear.

FF-Architekten Feldhusen & Fleckenstein

Intercultural Library at Kottbusser Tor

Berlin, Germany, *2010*

Located in a central traffic hub and multicultural area, this library reanimates an existing four-story building from the 1960's and provides a new attraction point for the bustling neighborhood. The luminous glass façade transforms the library into a glowing and welcoming beacon. A system of flexible glass partitions divide interior spaces while allowing for a constant stream of daylight to penetrate all areas of the building. Playful, colorful furniture animate the interior and offer a variety of seating arrangements for the curious.

*KARO**
Antje Heuer, Stefan Rettich
& Bert Hafermalz
Open-Air-Library

Magdeburg, Germany, *2009*

Inspired by the designer's temporary Open-Air-Library mock up that existed for just two days in an industrial site in East Germany, five years later, residents took it upon themselves to transform this project into a permanent, informal district library. An active collaboration between the designers and local residents, this outdoor library now hosts 30,000 books. The bookshelves are never closed, and all books are available to anyone that wants to use them. Lacking the bureaucracy and limited opening hours of its more formal counterparts, this flexible library adds a much-needed public space for residents while also rethinking the traditional, and often overly strict, model of the library.

Superpool
Open Library

Istanbul, Turkey, *2007*

The temporary transformation of an art-gallery space into a public reading room serves as a generous addition to the urban life of Istanbul's most crowded pedestrian street. Designed like an auditorium, seats run along one side of the gallery and backdrop of books on the other. This single space creates multiple opportunities for public interaction, including lectures, readings, and screenings. The mezzanine level above the gallery floor provides a private study zone for the more focused visitors in need of some quiet.

TYIN Tegnestue Architects

Safe Haven Library

Ban Tha Song Yang, Thailand, *2009*

This project is the result of a collaborative workshop between TYIN and 15 Norwegian architecture students at the Safe Haven Orphanage in Thailand. Completed in just two weeks, the library uses only local materials and labor. The walls consist of plastered concrete blocks that cool the building during the day. The simple construction of the open bamboo façades provide ample natural ventilation through out the entire structure. The solid-frame construction consists of iron wood, creating a comfortable floor for the children to play upon. Floor-to-ceiling bookshelves run across the full length of the concrete wall and the floor remains unfurnished to allow room for different activities. The entrance functions as a comfortable buffer zone between a small computer area on one side and a larger library room on the other. This inspiring library provides the children of the orphanage with a warm and protective space to read, study, and gather.

Fruits

V.

Off the Beaten Track

Playground

The ability and importance of the playground to evoke and maintain a sense of fun and a youthful attitude regardless of one's age should not be underestimated. While playgrounds are often associated with being exclusively for children, the cathartic outlet they offer to both the mind and body need not be limited to the young. The development of new models of the playground for young adults, adults, and seniors recaptures the playful nature of youth while simultaneously sharpening motor skills and one's imagination. In addition to the expansion of the playground to cater to different age groups, a rethinking of the traditional children's playground results in projects that inspire independence and increase creativity through the incorporation of design elements that readily engage the five senses. These showcased projects provide an overview of the most cutting-edge examples of new youth playgrounds and models for reintegrating fun into the realm of the adult.

ROBERT B. SAMUELS INC.
Licensed Electrical Contractor
212-645-5150

Rockwell Group
Imagination Playground

New York, USA, *2010*

The result of seven years of research, development, focus groups and testing, Imagination Playground stands as a breakthrough play-space concept that encourages child-directed, unstructured free play. With a focus on small, individual parts, this project offers a changing array of elements that allow children to constantly reconfigure their environment and design their own course of play. This unique playground provides a flexible environment for many types of imaginative activities through the incorporation of multilevel spaces with large sand and water features and a variety of toys and tools. The diverse design enables children to play intuitively as they build, tear down, and rebuild again. Elements including cascading water channels, climbing rope, masts and pulleys, and a lookout ramp with telescopes all work together to capture the rich maritime and commercial history of the playground's South Street Seaport location. To additionally reflect the proximity to the East River, buckets, sandbags, and wooden dams integrate into the play areas while seating and storytelling take place in the tiered steps of the amphitheater.

Carve with Marie-Laure Hoedemakers
Bijlmerpark

Amsterdam, Netherlands, *2011*

Located in the heart of central Amsterdam, this project comprises a park encircled by a central sports facility with residential units flanked along the sides. A sports and games esplanade in the center of the park offers a paved multipurpose sports court. A series of yellow frames mingle with a sparkling pink safety surface to create the main play strip containing a variety of rope bridges and a zip line which connects to a multilevel playing wall. Two rolling hills hover above the playing wall and the first houses a large skate park consisting of two connected pools. The second hill provides a colorful water and sand playground for the youngest children to enjoy.

Carve
Melis Stokepark

The Hague, Netherlands, *2010*

This playground consists of an ascending ring that doubles as both a curving route to the slide and a two-sided climbable boundary. Constructed out of strips of wood with perforations and round climbing holds, the vertical outer ring encloses an inner area with blue undulating playing slopes and a sandpit. Several passages lead to and from this inner area and offer their own seating and playing options. This private inner play area provides a secluded spot for children who have difficulties keeping up in the larger open spaces. The wooden wall with horizontal climbing routes and steep slopes provides a range of opportunities for play depending on the age and skill-set of each child.

Helen & Hard

Geopark

Stavanger, Norway, *2008*

Situated in the heart of Norway's oil industry, Geopark combines the expertise and material resources of the offshore rigs with sustainable urban development. The park provides a playful urban space on the waterfront, utilizing a vacant forecourt adjacent to the Oil Museum. Inspired by the most valuable Norwegian oil and gas reservoir, Troll, the topography of the park reflects the geological layers of this field at a scale of 1:500. This multipurpose geo-landscape accommodates biking, skating, climbing, exhibition, concerts, sports, and relaxation. Constructed out of recycled elements from petroleum installations, abandoned oil platforms, offshore bases, and scrap heaps, Geopark transforms the formerly abandoned site into a bustling social meeting point used by kids and adults alike.

Helen & Hard

Base Camp

Strand, Norway, *2009*

Base Camp introduces 12- to 15-year-old children to outdoor and camping activities through a dynamic architectural intervention. Comprised of interactive, nomadic structures, this project encourages children to play, learn, and explore. The camps derive their materiality and structure through a dialogue with the natural environment and constitute a playful praxis of place making. In Mountain Wall, children sleep inside a steel structure attached to a steep rock. The entire camp is hung on steel wires while pressure-loaded steel tubes create the distance between the rock and the camp's façade. These tubes double as bed frames, supporting five levels of sleeping platforms. A cotton, camouflage-painted sheath envelops the cabin, mimicking the rock beyond. Tree Camp consists of six cocoons hung around living trees, providing shelter for camping children. Four cocoons are connected by a hanging bridge, which leads into a larger pod where children can meet and prepare food. Water Camp houses children in hammocks on a covered quay. Built into the rock, this wheelchair accessible camp echoes the dramatic natural forces of the site.

Erect Architecture
Kilburn Grange Park Adventure Playcentre and Playground

London, UK, *2010*

This project comprises custom-designed internal and external spaces for play. Doubling as a center for special-needs children, the project also offers facilities for overnight stays. The playgrounds cultivate a unique and evolving relationship with children, encouraging participation, and empowering them to shape and develop their independent identities. Large roof overhangs create covered outdoor play space while the main part of the park consists of new topographies, landscapes, and site-specific climbing structures built around the existing trees. This unusual play center hosts a series of endless connections between spaces allowing for a lasting experience of discovery.

Erect Architecture

Found Sound, The Forest Playground, Old Ford Primary School

London, UK, *2008*

This experimental sound machine stands as the built result of a collaborative music workshop between the architects and a group of two-year-old children. The workshop taught the students how to collect and build objects to create a range of sounds that express their emotions. Based on these installations, the final design for this part of the playground suspends an assortment of found objects within a cube to define distinct emotional spaces. The open, happy space challenges children to jump in order to reach bright sounding objects while a low tunnel for anticipation fills with ambiguous sounds. This tunnel then opens into a tall, sombre, and calm space, complete with chair to contemplate a framed view of the trees and sky.

Erect Architecture
Evelyn Court Playground

London, UK, *2010*

Within an urban area previously lacking in usable public parks, this playground design opens up space for users of all age groups. The design comprises of a series of sliced mounds of differing characters which mediate between the existing levels. The mounds, made from solid earth forms, timber, or climbing nets, offer interesting spaces above, underneath, and in between for both play and socialising. These interstitial spaces also provide children with more traditional pieces of play equipment, developing incentive to imaginatively explore, inhabit and take ownership of the playground.

Monstrum
The Sperm Whale at the North Sea Oceanarium

Hirtshals, Denmark, *2008*

The first stage of a larger North Sea Oceanarium playground, this sperm whale serves as the central point for the project. The whale, which can be be traversed both inside and out, offers decorative drawings of its internal organs from within and glimpses of its white ribs along the side. Fitted with ladders, stairs, and other climbing areas, the whale can also be entered through the mouth across the teeth. Small holes run along the side of the whale doubling as both peepholes and climbing grips.

Monstrum

Rasmus Klump Land

Copenhagen, Denmark, *2010*

Located in the heart of Copenhagen in Tivoli, this play space takes its formal approach from the adventure stories of a Danish comic strip. The playground incorporates numerous water elements, maritime themes, and a large whale, around which many challenges and activities await. From rock hopping, to rope climbing, the project offers excitement for toddlers through adolescents.

Monstrum

The Parrot

Copenhagen, Denmark, *2009*

The central element of a Danish playground, this iconic parrot provides multiple levels of of indoor and outdoor play space. A large inclined deck covers the parrot's tail while the backside of the bird transitions into a slide.

playfit GmbH

playfit for the quality of life

More than 400 playfit locations across Europe

playfit caters to the enormous number of potential users who do not, or cannot, do very much exercise. This innovative product offers simple, low impact workouts for old and young alike. As all the equipment requires little effort to use, almost everyone becomes a viable candidate to begin improving health, mobility, flexibility, and co-ordination. This product not only promotes fitness but also social interaction between different generations.

C. F. Møller Architects

Aarhus Gymnastics and Motor Skills Hall

Aarhus, Denmark, *2010*

This unique sports hall serves children aged three to ten. The hall provides a giant activity landscape that motivates the kids to develop motor skills while having fun playing. A sculptural climbing frame rises in the middle of the hall and offers numerous sloping surfaces, holes, and hanging ropes to investigate. The many footbridges, platforms, trampolines, and pieces of jumping and climbing equipment all encourage and invite movement.

Numen / For Use
Net

Hasselt, Belgium, *2011*

This site-specific installation consists of system of flexible nets suspended in the air to form a floating landscape for visitors to climb in and explore. The parabolic layers of netting generate densities of light and dark spaces that constantly shift based on use. Resembling biomorphic architecture and urban utopias of previous decades, this project develops a spatially rich yet physically light structural network, offering a variety of spaces for fun, observation, and relaxation.

Tezuka Architects
Takaharu & Yui Tezuka
Woods of Net

Ninotaira, Japan, *2009*

This colorful, permanent pavilion serves as a tactile and whimsical children's play space. Designed for and hand knit by artist Toshiko Horiuchi Macadam, the project confounds distinctions between indoor and outdoor space. Suspended within a loosely stacked wooden structure, the main net space attracts children while their parents occupy the more understated wooden perimeter. Mixing cutting edge fabrication technology with traditional Japanese wood construction, this provocative project offers a refreshing and long-lasting alternative for rethinking standard designs for playground architecture.

Mathieu Lehanneur

Nouvel Atelier Des Enfants

Paris, France, *2010*

Located within the Centre Pompidou in Paris, this workshop provides space for individualized art education for children from two to twelve years old. The versatile facility uses plastic floors and walls and provides ample space for installations and dance practices. Within these spaces, workshops are conducted to encourage children to develop their powers of observation and imagination. These workshops welcome more than 23,000 children per year and enable them to experiment with a range of artistic techniques. The tactile and hands-on nature of this project promotes art education as a sensorial and integral part of cultural development.

Caterina Tiazzoldi,
Nuova Ordentra
& Benamor Duarte Architecture
# Onion Pinch

Lisbon, Portugal, *2009*

Appearing first in a Lisbon subway station and then moving across greater Europe, this organically shaped cork installation serves as a unique public playground for all ages. The flexibility of the cork results in a series of 15 tactile and dynamic pinched spaces that inspire user interaction and fluctuate between shelter, hammock, and open space. Internal paths between the onion profiles adds an additional pathway for children to run, walk, climb, lay and rock upon. The presence of these oscillating rings transforms unfamiliar and cold spaces into a lively oasis brimming with adults and children.

escuela

VI.

Communal Learning

Cultural Center

Community and cultural centers represent a generally underutilized, yet extremely valuable, public space for the continuation of learning outside of the school environment. These informal social settings offer invaluable resources to everyone from toddlers to senior citizens. Whether one needs a little extra support after class or takes up new hobbies upon retirement, these centers function as organic and adaptable public forums for exchanging information and strengthening social bonds. From dance center to ecological training facility, the projects explored here provide a holistic architectural approach that creates a safe haven for nurturing informal methods of both teaching and learning across generations.

FAXI

Henning Larsen Architects
& Batteriid Architects

Harpa – Reykjavik Concert Hall and Conference Centre

Reykjavik, Iceland, *2011*

This hall gathers its aesthetic inspiration from the northern lights and the dramatic Icelandic scenery. Situated on the border between land and sea, the project stands out as a large, radiant sculpture reflecting the surrounding sky, mountains, harbor space, and the vibrant life of the city. The impressive façades are the result of a close collaboration between between Henning Larsen Architects and the Danish-Icelandic artist Olafur Eliasson. The building features an arrival and foyer area, four performance halls, and an extensive backstage with offices, administration, rehearsal space, and changing room. The three large halls sit next to one other and offer public access on the south side and backstage access from the north. The fourth floor functions as a multipurpose hall with room for more intimate shows and banquets. Seen from the foyer, the halls form a mountain-like mass reminiscent of the basalt rock found along the Reykjavik coastline. At the core of the rock, the main concert hall reveals its interior as a red-hot center for musical expoloration.

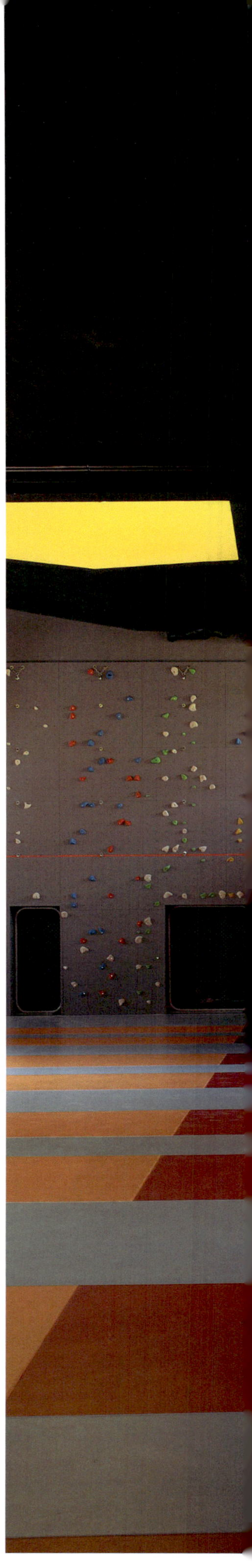

KOZ Architectes
Christophe Ouhayoun
& Nicolas Ziesel
Le Ruban

Saint-Cloud, France, 2009

This youth center and sports complex utilizes vibrant color coding and ample circulation paths to encourage independence by helping the children visually mark and identify their surroundings. With hallways spanning nearly three times their standard regulation sizes, the additional space allows for more informal gatherings, seating, and game areas. A rainbow beacon in an otherwise quiet Parisian-style neighborhood, this project evokes an impending sense of fun and curiosity.

Ecosistema Urbano
Ecopolis Plaza

Madrid, Spain, *2010*

Ecopolis Plaza transforms a faceless site in Madrid's urban sprawl into a public space for social interaction and a childcare center. This project incorporates the idea of sustainability into daily life, reducing energy consumption through its design, while simultaneously imparting awareness for sustainability to children at an early age. By burying half of the building and incorporating a large glass facade facing south, the architecture capitalizes on the land's thermal inertia and solar energy. A bioclimatic textile layer superimposed over a light steel structure serves as the interface between interior and exterior spaces. The building extends into the plaza where slides and play equipment are located for the children and provides a sheltered oasis from the surrounding industrial landscape.

3LHD Architects

Zagreb Dance Centre

Zagreb, Croatia, *2009*

Converted from an old movie theater, just 100 meters from the main square, this dance center provides a new home for Zagreb's 40 different contemporary dance troops. The project accommodates numerous dancers, choreographers, art troops, and companies with three multipurpose studios, spacious dressing rooms, offices, and prop storage. The entrance lobby serves as the only new architectural element in the center and provides a space for communication and meeting in addition to a cafe, library, and video store. The main volume and its broken form suggest dance movement while connecting the courtyard and roof terrace. This restored roof terrace stands as Zagreb's last extant open roof stage.

Yoshimasa Tsutsumi

Anzas Entertainment Dance Studio

Beijing, China, *2009*

This dance studio, wrapped in an ephemeral fog, confirms the movements of the body through the elegant use of mirrors with varied reflectivity. Creating a near whiteout state allows for the accentuation of the dark floor and the dancer's footwork. The application of a white-dot pattern onto the mirrors merges the floor far into the wall. The strategic and subtle blurring of everything but the floor results in a stunning dance studio continously bordering on the sublime.

BIG & JDS
Maritime Youth House

Copenhagen, Denmark, *2004*

Transforming a polluted site into an architectural playground, this project develops a dynamic maritime landscape open to the public for a range of social functions. Covering the site with a wooden deck actively contains the polluted soil, allowing project funds to be invested into the main building. Housing both a sailing club and youth center, the primary design strategy focuses on the resolution of their conflicting spatial requirements. While the youth center requires outdoor space to play, the sailing club takes up most of the site with mooring boats. The project addresses both groups by elevating the deck high enough to allow for boat storage underneath while the top surface forms an undulating landscape for the kids to run and play. This voluptuous wooden deck inventively supports the entirety of the Maritime Youth House's indoor and outdoor programmatic needs.

BIG & JDS

Sjakket Youth Center

Copenhagen, Denmark, *2007*

A converted factory turned community center, Sjakket provides Copenhagen's immigrant youth with a positive alternative to life on the streets. Situated in an industrialized immigrant neighborhood, the center functions as a safe haven to activate, educate, and inspire local youth. While the exterior gables and structural walls of the building are subject to strict preservation rules, the barrel-vaulted interiors accommodate both private program and a vast sports hall. On the roof, a half-pipe sundeck is wedged between the two vaults, resulting in a secret oasis for the kids. Accessed from this raised terrace, the sound studio bridges the vaults, announcing the center's presence amidst the industrial skyline. The southern vault opens to the courtyard beyond through large-scale garage doors that extend the interior into the urban realm. Sjakket integrates rather than alienates through the use of color, futuristic detailing, and connection to the surrounding community.

G. studio architects, Bruno Kubler landscape, Gettec, Jost, E3

Atelier au Terrain de Jeux et d'Aventures

Strasbourg, France, *2010*

This playground and adventure center provides a comfortable bright space for children to explore and engage in group and individual projects. Colorful panels on the building's façade create inviting visual markers to identify main entrance points. A fluid, ergonomic wooden interior opens into an outdoor activity terrace, allowing the children to engage with the interior and exterior of the project simultaneously.

Nieto Sobejano Arquitectos

Interactive Museum of the History of Lugo

Lugo, Spain, *2011*

A former industrial site turned thriving museum park, this project assimilates architecture directly into the landscape and links together a sequence of green areas in the city. The program divides into two large, connected areas: the partially buried parking structure and the visitor center and museum. The visitor center is organized within a single floor illuminated through large circular courtyards, allowing natural light to penetrate the space in independent, controlled instances. From the main courtyard, the most pronounced exhibition rooms emerge in the form of impressive, cylindrical bastions which house audiovisual installations and projections. Both the museum and visitor center offer an articulated sequence of interior and exterior spaces, engaging and building upon the user's connection to and awareness of the local environment.

Giancarlo Mazzanti
Jardín Social Timayui

Santa Marta, Colombia, *2010*

This futuristic project stands as the result of a collective effort made by the local municipality of Santa Marta and the Carulla Foundation to improve the educational and nutritional conditions of communities displaced by violence. The Jardín Social Timayui develops infrastructure to improve the dietary and psychomotor conditions of children aged from zero to five years old, living in low-income neighborhoods. Spread across a pristine green field, these geometric campus modules provide a safe haven filled with light, community, and hope.

NSMH
Yahsibey Summer School

Yahsibey, Turkey, 2006

This summer school is located in a small Aegean village with a bird's-eye view of the sea. Designed to blend in with the local vernacular, the buildings for this summer school integrate the traditional stone walls with the exterior that offer privacy from the street and a plentiful garden space within. Developed for short-term workshops and summer schools, the project grows out of two primary masses; one for accommodation and the other for workspace. The two buildings open onto a shared courtyard, transforming them into a single, continuous space consisting of closed and open areas. This multipurpose indoor and outdoor project provides a flexible setting to host a range of activities and workshops.

BaO architects
Split Bathhouse

Shanmen, China, *2011*

Located in a rural area lacking basic hygienic amenities and public gathering spaces, this bathhouse doubles as a community center serving more than 5,000 adults and 1,000 children from the surrounding region. Conceived as an incubator of social, cultural, sanitary, environmental, and economic change, the project comprises two distinct buildings, one for men and one for women that are linked by a communal greenhouse. The two inverted main blocks, lined with windows to illuminate and ventilate the interiors, extend from the central greenhouse and contain green and a yellow bathing spaces. Long benches surround both buildings providing seating for the greenhouse area. Encouraging public expression and a playful relationship with the architecture, the exterior walls are covered with blackboards for the exchange of information, drawings, and games. This simple yet engaging envelope results in a building that is continuously transforming and evolving with the interaction and creativity of its users.

TAXI
H2O
携
手
保

山门澡堂

Architects Rudanko & Kankkunen
Vocational Training Centre

Sra Pou, Cambodia, *2011*

This colorful vocational training center and community building teaches poor Cambodian families how to earn their own living. Built in an area lacking in basic infrastructure, a decent built environment, and access to secure income, this vocational school provides professional training and helps local residents start sustainable businesses together. Constructed from local materials with a local workforce, the project doubles as an architectural demonstration for the community, showing simple and transferable construction techniques using readily available elements. Made from sun dried soil blocks, the school was constructed entirely by hand. Small holes penetrate the soil bricks, allowing indirect sunlight and gentle wind to flow through the interior spaces. Colorful, handcrafted doors can be seen from a distance, welcoming visitors approaching from the main road.

24h Architecture
Maartje Lammers, Boris Zeisser, Olav Bruin & Anne Laure Nolen

Ecological Children Activity and Education Center

Koh Kood, Thailand, *2009*

Located within a hotel resort on an island in the Gulf of Thailand, this center offers visiting children a range of entertaining activities while cultivating ecological awareness. The project includes an auditorium for films, lectures, and plays, a library with books on permaculture and local traditions, and separate rooms for art, music, and fashion. Located on a rocky slope near the sea, the bamboo dome derives its formal inspiration from the manta ray. The structure and roof are made from local Thai bamboo while the wood for the interior comes from a nearby plantation. Sleeping pods for toddlers, a cooking cave, and a vegetable garden where children can learn to prepare their own meals all cluster around the exterior of the building. The roof cantilevers up to eight meters, providing shade and protection from the heavy rains, while the open design allows for natural airflow and minimal use of artificial lighting.

PT Bamboo Pure

Green School Bridge

Bali, Indonesia, *2007*

Located along a stunning river valley in Bali, Indonesia, this series of buildings advocates for the use of bamboo as a viable and sustainable alternative to rain forest timber as a primary building material. PT Bamboo's school demonstrates how to build with renewable materials, inspire and educate children to live sustainably, and motivates communities to fight climate change and poverty. To build such a project, three collaborative entities were created: Green School, PT Bamboo Factory, and the Bamboo Community Project. Green School functions as an educational institute where children learn about environmental practices, renewable energy, aquaculture, and organic farming. This project also trains local communities in the production and incorporation of bamboo into their everyday lifestyle and architecture. PT Bamboo serves as an efficient and progressive model for both sustainable learning and architectural expression.

VII.

Break out Sessions

Corporate Spaces

Bringing play into the workplace stands as perhaps the most significant breakthrough in the professional sphere and benefits both employers and employees equally. By integrating play, spontaneity, and a sense of fun into one's work, the boosting of employee morale and efficiency can happen almost simultaneously. As a happy and engaged workforce makes for a productive workforce, a rapid redesign of the traditional office space reflects this changing approach to the professional environment. This section shows a diverse assortment of corporate headquarters, offices, think tanks, breakout spaces, and laboratories that help keep work interesting through the development of dynamic environments that inspire both the mind and body. Through the incorporation of slides, flexible meeting spaces, access to the outdoors, and relaxation areas, these projects instill a sense of wonder and excitement into the world of work.

architecturespossibles
Christian Pottgiesser

Forest Through the Table

Paris, France, 2006

This surreal office space accommodates the headquarters of the Paris-based companies PONS and HUOT. Seven individual spaces for each director, one larger open office for employees, and a communal meeting and recreation room are strategically interspersed between lush vegetation. Converted from a dilapidated, industrial nineteenth-century hall, the project consists of a massive solid oak unit, with individual workplaces enclosed in Plexiglas cut from it. The meeting room, recreational room, and restrooms are all embedded within the solid areas of the wooden slab. The remaining areas in the platform house heating, water, and electrical appliances in addition to 18.3 cubic meters of soil for the eight Ficus Panda trees spread across the space. This project rethinks the parameters needed for a successful and inspiring work environment while providing an inventive architectural solution for reconnecting to nature.

Mathieu Lehanneur
LaboBrain

Paris, France, *2008*

The LaboBrain serves as a custom-made studio for David Edwards, the founder of Laboratoire. Designed as a gymnasium and training space for cultivating thought, the project encourages constant movement by providing different surfaces for drawing and sketching, rather than a singular static work area. Merging science, art and design with a love for Buckminster Fuller, a geodesic, half-deflated, giant, leather soccer ball offers a place to rest and pay homage to the great architect and inventor between brainstorming sessions. The rational organization of the assistant's office furniture caters to the linear and orderly right side of this project's brain and provides a wall of immaculate white cardboard boxes for use as paper archives.

Albert France-Lanord Architects
Pionen – White Mountain

Stockholm, Sweden, *2010*

Located 30 meters below the granite rocks of the Vita Berg Park in Stockholm, this project transforms a former 1200 square meter anti-atomic shelter into a striking office and server storage space for a local internet provider. Without access to direct sunlight, interior lighting becomes one of the most important and challenging aspects of the project, requiring as much variation as possible to help prevent users from losing track of time. Inspired by classic science fiction films and Kevin Adam's set design for James Bond, the project fluctuates between rooms where human intervention acts as the prevailing design feature and rooms simply dominated by the rock.

Elding Oscarson
No Picnic

Stockholm, Sweden, *2011*

This light-filled office houses one of the world's largest design consultant agencies. The project encompasses open office areas, a prototype workshop and show-room, several project rooms, and a striking customer area. Located within two nineteenth-century buildings under strict historic preservation regulations, the conversion for this project utilizes a sensitive and minimally invasive design strategy. The first building, restored to its prior glory, remains virtually unchanged except for the addition of a customized acoustic treatment along the walls. The second building, however, integrates a delicate, aluminium wall into the space to create a mirroring effect that unifies the otherwise visually lopsided room. The meeting rooms are located inside this metal membrane and boast large windows facing the hall. These transparent glass planes combined with the opaque aluminium surface result in a space of visual illusion, where partitions and openings appear and disappear simultaneously .

Taranta Creations
Red Town Office Space

Shanghai, China, *2010*

A metal factory turned office for designers, this unusual intervention provides an adaptable space that supports a range of informal functions and reflects the company's experimental creative process. Needing to provide two floors of workspace in a structure only capable of accommodating one, a single, continuous, elevated platform offers a large, open work floor for designers to think, sketch, meet, draft, model, and relax. Within this platform, four recessed stations are cut from it to provide more traditional workspaces. A central staircase, reminiscent of a large droplet of water, produces a highly saturated, bright red transitional space between office areas. This progressive interpretation of space encourages cross-collaboration between different projects and disciplines within the studio.

Electric Dreams
Fabricville

Gothenburg, Sweden, *2010*

Inspired by the aesthetic of traditional Swedish wooden cottages and the organic organization of small villages, this project gathers a number of fashion brands, each with different spatial requirements and design values, under one roof. Originally divided into several offices with different tenants, Fabricville reconnects the building into one three-floor headquarters. The once long, narrow, and anonymous corridors now function as vibrant streets merging workshops for the clothing designers, offices for the marketing people, and brightly colored, indoor conference rooms for meetings. Each floor offers a different color scheme to match the identity of the brand located on its level, resulting in a collective atmosphere of individuality, connectivity, and fun.

i29
Office 03

Amsterdam, Netherlands, *2009*

This grey and white office space, designed to last only two years, focuses on the principle of doing more with less. By spray painting a collection of second-hand and reused furniture in an identical finish, the project brings new life to otherwise mundane furnishings and through color unifies them into a visually striking, unified workspace. To accentuate the monolithic character of the matte-colored furniture, grey squares are painted on the concrete floor to frame the different areas in the office. Reception, working stations, lounge areas, and canteen are all integrated into this minimalist design concept and can be easily expanded or reduced once the company relocates to a new headquarters.

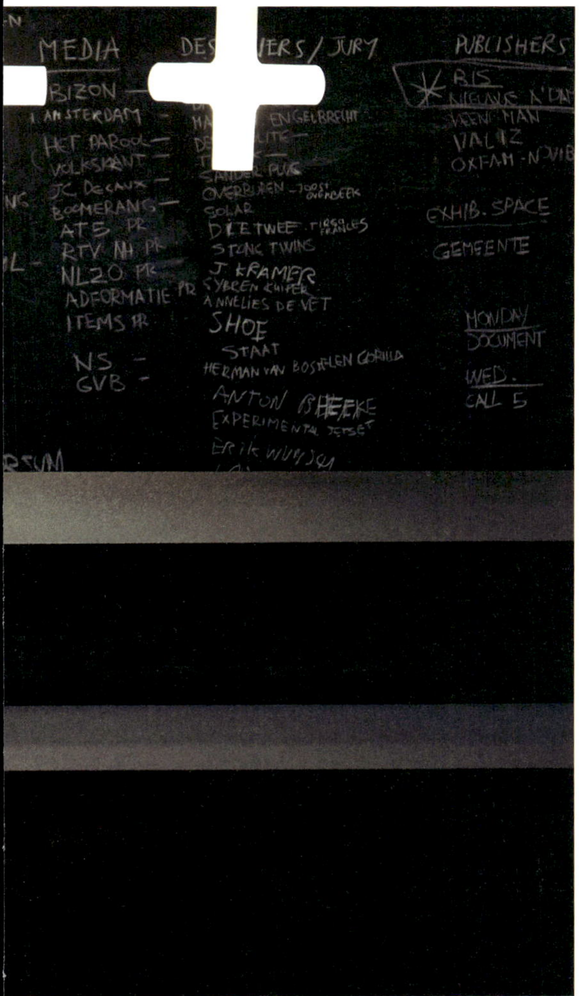

i29

Office 04

Amsterdam, Netherlands, *2011*

This new office for a highly ranked digital marketing agency encourages creative interaction through the use of flexible work stations and communal open spaces. Serving as both a headquarters and brand identity, the design of this office reflects the agency's friendly, playful, and professional personality. Dark grey felt blankets the floors, ceilings, walls, and furniture, producing both a visually striking office identity and an effective strategy for sound absorption which allows for a sense of privacy within larger open areas.

Cedric Bomford & Elke Reichel Architekten
Dorten Office

Stuttgart, German, *2011*

The intimate yet expansive new headquarters for a German communications agency doubles as both an adventurous playground and innovative work space. Providing a series of larger and smaller spaces for meeting, discussing, and thinking, this hand-crafted, project straddles the intersections of architecture, design, and art.

BuroKoek

New Office Space of Recycled Wood

's-Hertogenbosch, *2010*

Under tight time constraints to relocate after this Dutch design agency's office was sold much quicker than expected, the team completed this custom built work space in under six weeks. Made of recycled wood panels and cement fiber, a soundproof meeting room serves as a focal point for the new office. The exterior of this meeting space integrates an inventive and efficient system for shelving and storage, resulting in increased functionality and an aesthetically optimized design element for the space.

Alexis Dornier
Made Space

Berlin, Germany, *2010*

This gallery and studio space for creative collaborations offers a series of programmatic and infrastructural elements that accommodate an adaptable, project-based workflow. A flexible hardscape comprising tables, chairs, movable walls, and storage doubles as the core spatial element for the studio. This central core enables the rapid reconfiguration of lounge furniture, low tables, and the bar area, activating the space during events and collaborations. An array of customized light fixtures cover the ceiling, creating a flexible and infinitely adaptable spatial environment.

Studio Makkink & Bey

Reception Space – Department of Tourism

Apeldoorn, Netherlands, 2007

Using a light blue and white color palette, this unusual reception area evokes a sense of freshness and cleanliness. A selection of stylized images of people, plants, and texts relating to tourism cover the floors, walls, furniture, and curtains, producing a graphic and flexible interior landscape. The texts positioned at the top of the curtain partitions appear to float, mimicking clouds in a great blue sky. The more intimate discussion areas are furnished with rocking chairs to create a relaxed situation that encourages dialogue.

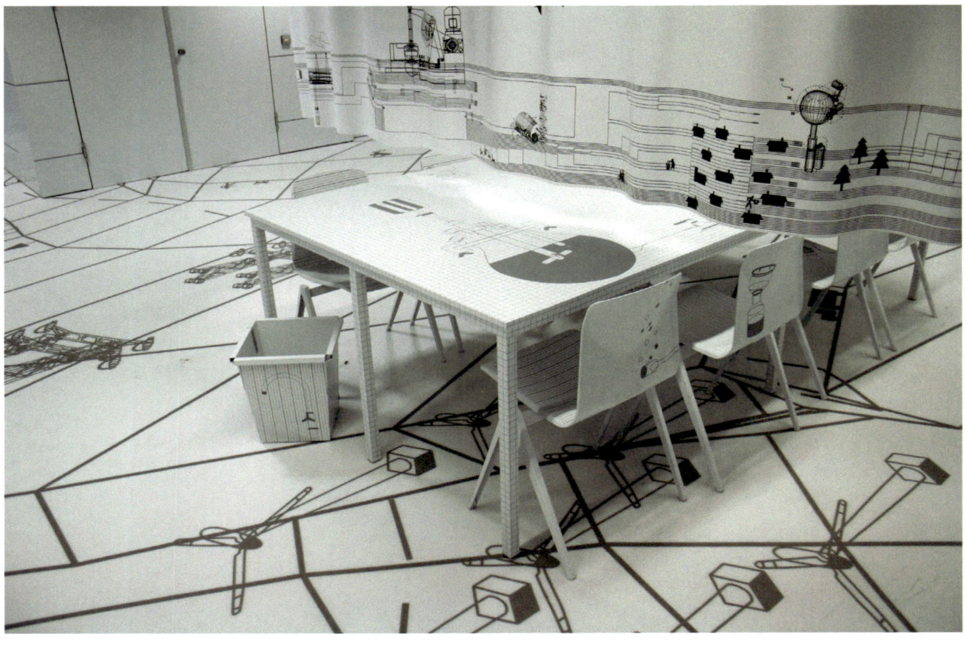

Studio Makkink & Bey
with Eric Klarenbeek
Work Sofa

Netherlands & Belgium, *2008*

Displayed at the Interieur Biennale, this innovative product upends standard conceptions of what furniture should look like and how it can behave. While in a standard couch one's seating choices prove relatively limited, with Work Sofa's movable components allow for a seemingly limitless number of modifications. The angular sofa functions like a giant puzzle, providing seating options to facilitate conferencing, collaborative working, and privacy.

Total Tool BA
Urban Station

Buenos Aires, Argentina, *2010*

Conceived as a hybrid space that combines café with a temporary office, this project caters to a clientele of nomadic workers. Urban Station reconsiders the traditional typology of the café as workplace by adding custom-designed office amenities including tables specially adapted for laptops, private meeting rooms with projectors and video-conference equipment, and a help desk for printing and errand services. From the organization of promotional events to free bicycles available for borrowing during breaks, additional adjunct services provide enhanced comfort and opportunities for interaction. Conceived as a franchise with more than three new branches to be completed by December 2011, the flagship store of Urban Station functions as a new prototype for merging café culture with a productive work environment.

Uuushh – Andrea Paoletti
The Hub Rovereto

Rovereto, Italy, *2011*

Transforming an art gallery into an unique space for innovation, this headquarters functions as a member's club, innovation agency, office, and think-tank. The project's design reflects the agency's dedication to invention and entrepreneurship through the incorporation of mixed workstations that gather people in fluid configurations to encourage collaborative thinking. Designed to build members' excitement and inspire creativity in their work, the Hub serves as a timeshare workspace that can be converted into a social and cultural meeting area. Visitors and members are guided into the space by evocative phrases written on the perimeter walls. Modular furniture allows for a flexible work flow to accommodate individual desks, a larger conference room, or a projection area. The Hub offers inspired places for meeting, working, learning, creating, and connecting.

Creation
Center

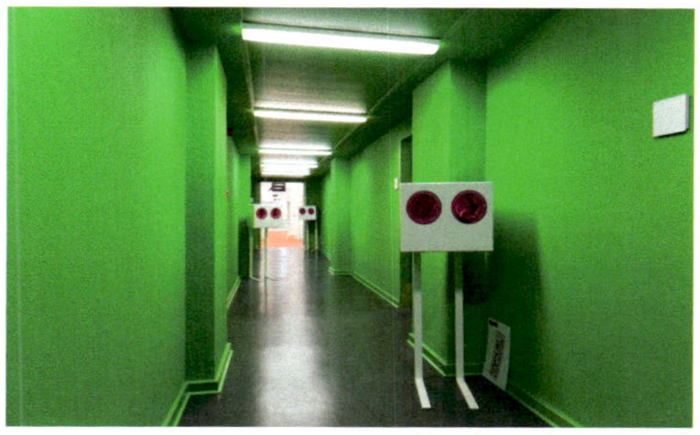

Telekom Laboratories **Creation Center**

Berlin, Germany, *2010*

The Creation Center functions as a conceptual and physical platform for innovation. Providing a tangible, methodological framework to spark and promote creativity, multidisciplinary workshops focus on design thinking, stimulating participants' creative potential and generating new ideas. Aiming to find inspiration for future digital communication services and product ideas, interdisciplinary creative teams work in spaces tailored to the cultivation of a successful innovation process. The application of bright colors in the offices nurtures an atmosphere for experimentation and visually divides the space into distinctive areas for work, lounge, play, and meeting. Flexibility, light, and communal areas all work together to ensure a lively space for creative thinking.

Rosan Bosch & Rune Fjord
Lego PMD

Billund, Denmark, *2010*

This headquarters for LEGO boasts a physical working environment that corresponds to its playful products. Offering a unique development department where the designers can become part of the children's fantasy world, this imaginative project provides a work space that prioritizes fun, play, and creativity in its adult employees. An existing walkway transforms into an oversized seating area which then expands into sofas and a slide connecting the two floors. A large open space on the ground floor creates a dynamic meeting place for socializing and exchanging information. A fun zone with a yellow bar encourages relaxation, while a number of building tables for children make it possible for the company's youngest employees to test the newest models and products. Notions of scale are repeatedly challenged through the use of giant graphics of grass for the walls, an oversized legoman, and tables filled with built-in bonsai gardens. These tricks in perception and scale question one's understandings of who is big and who is small and blurs the line between work and imagination.

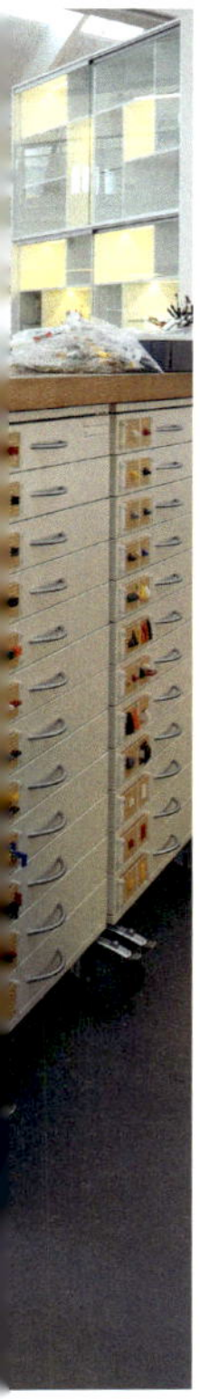

Blitz

Skype North American Headquarters

Palo Alto, USA, *2010*

Desiring a headquarters that would distinguish the Skype brand from its competition, this space reflects the company's spirit of innovation in a highly functional yet creative workplace designed to encourage interaction and spontaneity. To support agility and innovative thinking, a mix of environments facilitate collaboration, contemplation, and concentration. The concentration zones represent the workstation areas and reside along the building perimeter, benefiting from natural light and lower noise levels. Collaboration zones where meeting rooms, coffee kiosks, and whiteboard areas cluster, are centered along main access spines on each level to encourage socialization. Contemplation spaces take the shape of casual lounges. A system of mobile whiteboards, or 'Skype-Its' and meeting pods are deployed throughout the space to capture ideas as they occur. A simple color palette uses ordinary materials in new and creative ways, uniting and familiarizing the largely open warehouse workspace.

How Asia Advertises

Hassell
dtac House

Bangkok, Thailand, *2009*

Housing one of Thailand's leading telecommunication providers, this project accommodates 3,500 staff over 20 floors in a massive 62,000-square-meter building. Dtac's philosophy of "play and learn" successfully imbeds itself into the design of this workplace, challenging conventional notions of arrival, meeting, concentration, and relaxation spaces. To support the companies numerous promotional activities, an extensive three-level room linked by an internal stairway provides a highly adaptable space, capable of hosting a wide variety of client and staff events. With spaces defined as volumes rather than by function, the rich and versatile use of local timbers for the flooring, screening, and ceiling details define direction and framework across this activity-based workplace. The collaborative environment encourage staff mobility and creativity while the incorporation of a dedicated relaxation and fitness floor promotes physical health as an integral component of a productive workflow.

Hassell
ANZ Centre

Melbourne, Australia, *2010*

ANZ Centre, located in Melbourne's Docklands, applies a contemporary perspective on workplace design that reflects the client's focus on engagement and productivity. The design evolves from the concept of an urban campus, applying the typology of the central common as the driving design parameter with a hierarchy of shared spaces extending from it. The openness and variation of the layout combined with the application of bold colors and dynamic vistas encourage interaction and participation. The ANZ Centre provides a total net area of 83,600 square meters over 13 levels, with floor plates ranging from 9,800–6,600 square meters. Configured to maximize natural daylight while promoting workplace integration, communication, and flexibility, ANZ Centre is the largest single-tenanted commercial office building in Australia.

Emmanuelle Moureaux Architecture & Design
Sugamo Shinkin Bank – Shimura branch

Tokyo, Japan, *2011*

This dazzling rainbow credit union produces a playful, light-filled graphic atmosphere. The exterior of the building integrates 12 layers of stacked rainbow colored planes that peek out from the façade to welcome visitors. Upon entering the bank, three elliptical skylights bathe the interior in a soft, diffused light, evoking a sense of openness and connection to the outdoors. Adorned with dandelion graphics that seem to float and drift through the air, the main ceiling dissolves into the lightness of the surrounding space. ATMs, teller windows, consultation booths, and an open waiting area are located on the first floor while the second story houses offices, meeting rooms, and a cafeteria. Three long glass air wells thread through the first and second levels of the building, flooding the interior with natural light and ventilation and creating an uplifting space for both customers and employees to enjoy.

C. F. Møller Architects
Second phase of the Darwin Centre

London, UK, *2008*

Showcasing and protecting the museum's collection, this massive cocoon-like form functions as an inner protective envelope for the building.The structure produces an icon for the center that directly references its connection to nature. Finished in an ivory-colored polished plaster, the organic form resembles a silk cocoon. The project serves as both a physical and metaphorical bridge between past, present, and future as it links between the original museum building and its more contemporary addition.

DC 619D
Entomology
DNA Extraction

Rojkind Arquitectos
Nestlé Innovation Lab

Queretaro, Mexico, *2009*

This project serves as a laboratory for the development of new products, a packaging center, and a satellite office. Inspired by strict building requirements which required the new building to have an arched porch, the project incorporates a series of intersecting spheres to create a continuous open portico. The areas housing the specific program requirements for the lab are comprised of orthogonal boxes clad in satin-mirrored glass. The opaque, metallic, and impenetrable appearance of the exterior actively contrasts with the brightly colored, vaulted interior spaces. The result of this series of visual and spatial contrasts results in a dynamic work environment that provides employees with a cheerful and unique sense of place.

Riken Yamamoto & Field Shop
Namics Techno Core

Niigata, Japan, *2008*

A research laboratory for a developer and manufacturer, the project dedicates its ground floor to experimental laboratory rooms. A green roof provides researchers with access to a garden and outdoor space while simultaneously decreasing strain on the building's cooling system. The building's structure consists of a series of reversed cones, also referred to as tops, in varying thicknesses. In this system, every three tops are gathered to support each other. Connecting tops with different diameters results in a table-like structural body that can then be stacked to accommodate multiple levels. With no exterior pillars, the unusual structure of this building allows it to appear infinitely light, resulting in a work space exuding elegance and a constant sense of wonder.

Dan Pearlman
MTV Headquarters

Berlin, Germany, *2010*

Inspired by the graphic identity of the MTV Networks (Germany), the interior design and material selections for the reception area, lobby, cafe, and atrium, reflect the font and autumnal color palette of the logo. In contrast, the design and diversity of layouts and work stations located within the communal, living-room spaces reference the dynamism and creativity of the city of Berlin. The accentuated use of color creates lively, themed meetings, and recreational rooms that inspire and revitalize employees. Accentuated by the use of abstract tree parasols and shades of green, the central atrium functions as an interior, collective garden serving as a pleasant refuge for employees to gather and relax.

VIII.

Meaningful Distractions

Installations

The rise of public installations offers an exciting platform for ongoing participating in lifelong learning. These unscripted spaces provide users with unique opportunities to perceive one's surrounding in new ways and engage with one's neighbors through the encouragement of spontaneous situations. The creation of these informal gatherings allows people that would otherwise remain forever strangers to sit, stand, or lay next to one another and share a common experience. This final grouping of projects demonstrates the tactile, interactive, and social components underlying the success of some of our favorite and unexpected spaces for extended education.

Faulders Studio
BAMscape

Berkeley, CA, *2010*

Merging the disciplines of art, architecture, and furniture design, BAMscape functions as a free-form public seating environment commissioned by the Berkeley Art Museum / Pacific Film Archive. Installed for a two-year duration, BAMscape provides a new centerpiece within the museum's large 6,692-square-foot central atrium gallery. To maximize volumetric presence within the budget limitations, the prefab system deploys CNC large-scale laser cutting processes to custom manufacture 150 individual curved modules. Lightweight and comprised of 93 percent air, the rigid-foam structural substrate is then laminated with thin layers of painted plywood. BAMscape hosts wireless Internet and integrated outlets for powering laptops, and allows visitors to enjoy the space as a site for study and social networking. An open area for lounging, film screenings, live performance, and multimedia events, BAMscape fosters the museum's practice of providing diverse event programming amidst its gallery spaces.

AHMET ÖĞÜT
EXPLODED CITY

Ball-Nogues Studio
Liquid Sky

New York City, USA, *2007*

The winning installation for the eighth annual MoMA/ P.S.1 Young Architects Program, Liquid Sky occupied the P.S.1 courtyard for the summer of 2007. Mixing a rich palette of atmospheric effects and brilliant colors with an undertone of circus spectacle results in an immersive environment saturated in kaleidoscopic patterns of color. An array of translucent, tinted petals resembling blossoming flowers of stained glass filter light across the space. The petals form a tensioned matrix that reconfigures the horizon, cresting above the walls of the courtyard and making the project visible from the surrounding streets. Six tripod towers constructed from untreated utility poles support the petals while providing discrete spaces at their base for relaxing on enormous community hammocks made of brightly colored netting.

*O*GE Architects*
Merav Eitan & Gaston Zahr

Giant Birdsnest for Breeding New Ideas

Haifa, Israel, *2009*

Conceived and executed by O*GE as a prototype for a new and inspiring socializing space, this project oscillates between furniture and playground. The largest nest, 4.50m in diameter, can host up to 16 people at once, offering a comfortable environment to host informal meetings in a variety of seating configurations. The simple, cozy, and visually enticing nest encourages visitors to climb in and play, relax, work, or exchange ideas.

KIT Universität Karlsruhe
Fachgebiete Tragkonstruktionen
& Building Lifecycle Management
Roll-It – Guerilla Housing

Karlsruhe, Germany, *2009*

Created by students from the University of Karlsruhe, this project presents a flexible and unusual living and working solution that capitalizes on its minimal interior. The cylinder-shaped space changes its function depending on its orientation as it rolls between workspace, bed, kitchen, and bath. The experimental design consists of an outer shell comprising four supporting rings, a torsion inner shell membrane, and thin external wooden slats which allow the running surface to roll and stop depending on one's preferred action within the space.

Dan Pearlman
Elise's Island

Berlin, Germany, *2009*

This collaboration between architects and physicians results in a space that promotes an emotionally positive healing process for children and adolescents. A hospital lacking the characteristic hostile, clinical atmosphere, this project instead introduces playful colors, organic shapes, soft materials, and light. Elise's Island satisfies medical standards of care while integrating an additional aesthetic and spatial intervention to address children's emotional needs, helping them develop a sense of community and identity.

Caterina Tiazzoldi – Interaction Design with Mirko Arcese & Luca Biada
The Social Cave

Milano, Italy, *2011*

This installation serves as part of the celebration of the 50th anniversary of the Milano furniture fair. Developed by a group of designers and 24 students, the Cave blends the frenzied excitement of virtual connectivity's power and speed with the weight of a parametric aggregation of 100 percent recycled foam cubes. Two enclosures separated by a barrier initially conceal visitors inhabiting each space from each other. The presence of a visitor in the opposite space reveals itself only through a projection capturing their movements. The physical anonymity created by the enclosure allows each visitor the privacy to engage in a digital and visual conversation with the projected shadow of their neighbor. First hiding and then exposing the proximity and identity of its visitors, this project initiates a conversation that transcends traditional digital and physical boundaries.

Ball-Nogues Studio
Rip Curl Canyon

Houston, Texas, *2006*

Commissioned as part of a collaboration between Rice Gallery and The Museum of Fine Art's exhibition, "The Modern West: American Landscape, 1890-1950," this installation challenges conventional interpretations of landscape and geological phenomenon. Fabricated out of laminated cardboard walls, a series of undulating ottomans inspire physical participation. This traversable rolling playground extends the casual social terrain of the Rice University campus into the gallery. On any given day one might discover a group of gallery goers studying, napping, climbing up or sliding down the rolling surfaces. Rip Curl Canyon represents a type of mythical location in the American West where land and water collide, far from Houston's flat drained swamps. Like rip currents – narrow, fast moving belts of water – the cardboard segments twist and surge toward the front glass entry wall. The view through the glass provides only glimpses of the unfolding topography, inviting curious visitors to probe deeper.

Aaron Jones
YouTube Theater

Detroit, USA, *2011*

Developed on the assumption that the internet can potentially deliver information anywhere, this outdoor pavilion functions as both a public theatre and classroom. A ground plane curved on one side provides users with a comfortable area to lounge while they enjoy their videos. The structure, comprised of post-processed, interlocking chain link fence components, allows the pavilion to be erected in a single day, referencing the rapid pace and development of the technology it displays.

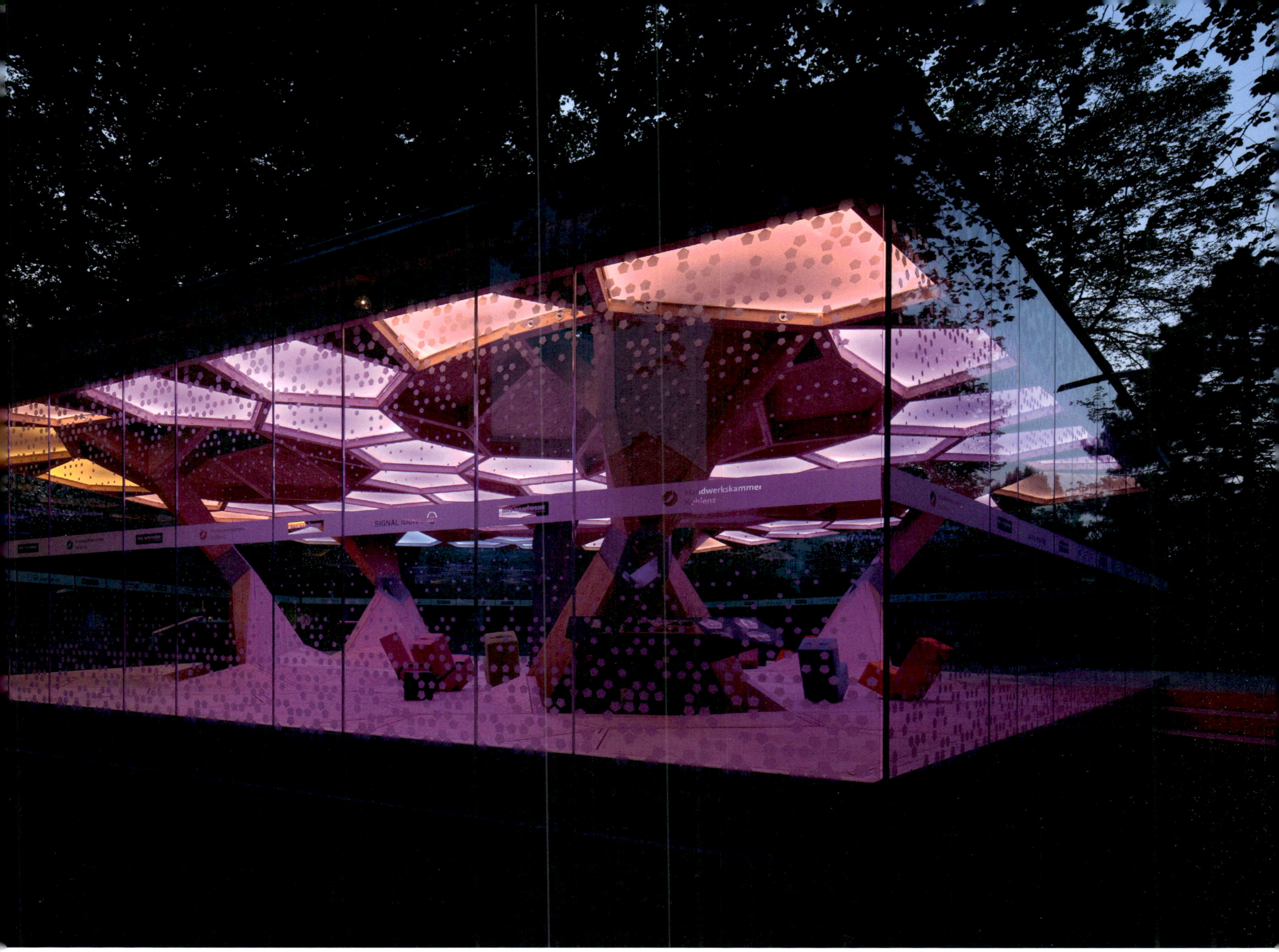

one fine day & FH Trier

Treehugger

Koblenz, Germany, *2011*

Located between a group of Linden trees, this former parking lot turned pavilion creates a dynamic and engaging site for local residents to gather. Formally and spatially eye catching, the project presents a site-specific installation that also doubles as a working architectural prototype. A matrix of pentagonal wooden modules form the ceiling, allowing one of the large trees on the site to become the focal point at the center of the space. The distortion of this ceiling grid establishes five connections between the floor and roof, providing room for skylights while also evoking a sensation of occupying a space underneath a great tree canopy. The combination of methodical structural analysis with a playful approach to surrounding context results in a space where visitors can connect with nature, architecture, and one another.

KidsPatch
KidsPatch Mini-Lab

Majdanpek, Serbia, *2011*

KidsPatch functions as a children's mini-festival providing a series of activities in the fields of contemporary music, graphic art, performance, and new media. A 100 percent participatory program, this project establishes a two-way creative process and exchange between participating children and the artists guiding the workshops. Throughout these courses, children learn new skills for developing their individual approach to the creative process. The results of these workshops present themselves immediately in the form of concerts, exhibitions, activity areas, installations, performances, and screenings. Tailored to each location and context, the programs focus on children from the ages of five to twelve. Since 2008, KidsPatch presented an annual festival event in its hometown of Belgrade while also reaching out to locations around the world including Poland, Austria, Slovenia, Serbia, and the USA.

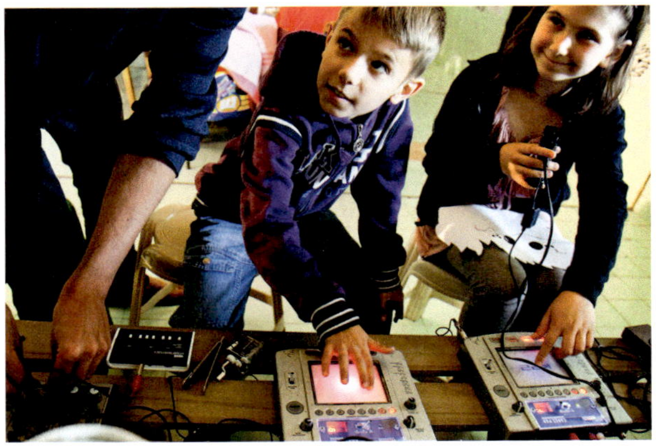

Dis-patch Collective
ViceVerse Residency

Majdanpek, Serbia, *2011*

Establishing an unusual and challenging context for collaborative and creative investigation, this project experiments with the notion of artistic focus and exchange. A group of 15 authors and students spent four days transforming this unfinished, abandoned house next to a secluded lake into a temporary lab filled with life and creativity. Reflecting on the conflicting beauty of the surrounding nature juxtaposed with the brutal realities of the nearby mining town, participants produced a 32-page handcrafted magazine to detail their experience.

Harry Gugger & Leopold Banchini

Reclaim

Venice, Italy, *2010*

Inspired by the dramatic urbanization of the Bahraini coastline, Reclaim uses the setting of the Venice Biennale to investigate the socio-political changes that have lead to the dramatic transformation of this nation that once brimmed with fishers and pearl divers. The decline of maritime culture in favor of a more generic urban lifestyle provoked the designer's to install three original, displaced, fishermen huts into the exhibition space. These humble, and nearly forgotten, homes offer visitors the chance to both visually experience and spatially learn about a lost way of living, ever connected to the sea.

1/100
Leopold Banchini
Nomad

Paris, France, *2011*

Most recently found occupying the gardens of the Musée du quai Branly in Paris, this lightweight and mobile nomadic installation comprises a collection of caravans, tents, carpets and stools meant to inspire and promote interaction and spatial awareness. Enabling the domestication and the appropriation of multiple garden spaces, five informal settlements provide platforms for events, socialization, and subsistence. Redesigned second-hand caravans offer shelter for an information area, sound-system, and ice cream van. Agricultural canvas fixed to the caravans creates shade while a floor full of colorful carpets invites visitors to linger. Lightweight foldable wood furniture inspired from the museum collections weaves through the site, reintegrating these prized gallery objects back into everyday life.

Assemble
Folly for a Flyover
London, UK, *2011*

Transforming the cavernous space located underneath a major London overpass in a thriving public space, this project hosts a six-week summer program of waterside cinema, performance, and play. Hand built with local, reclaimed, and donated materials, the Folly draws inspiration from the surrounding red-brick buildings, posing as an imaginary piece of the area's past, a building trapped under the motorway. By day, the site houses a café, workshops, events, and local boat trips. At night, screenings ranging from animation classics to early and experimental cinema with live scores, light shows, and performances transform the site into a dynamic open-air theatre space.

Atelier Bow-Wow

BMW Guggenheim Lab

New York City, USA, *2011*

The first stop in a nine-city tour, this mobile and temporary laboratory stands as the result of a collaborative effort between the Guggenheim Museum and BMW to create a contemporary public forum for lively dialogue. The collapsible structure accommodates numerous public events including film screenings, lectures, and workshops. Screens and furniture attach to tracks on the frame allowing for constant rearranging, while white curtains span the full length of the space to create partitions as needed. A tent made of a carbon fiber frame clad in layers of mesh fabric, this migrating pavilion operates as a engaging urban playhouse for the communities it visits.

Institute of Play
SMALLab at Play

New York City, USA, *2010–2011*

Frac Attack (1)
A relay race game and engaging math experiment, this project lets teams of players help programmers debug complex code by finding the lowest common denominators for increasingly difficult fraction pairs.

Kalc's Safe (2)
This project uses motion-capture cameras, short-throw projectors, and wireless controllers to immerse players in dynamic game-based scenarios where they can interact with each other and digital game elements in real time within shared physical space. The scenarios bring learning to life by engaging kids in full-body physical activity. All scenarios support situated learning, large-group participation, team work, complex problem solving, and fun physical activity. This game teaches children techniques to intuitively master the measurement of angles. Players must break into a virtual bank safe secured with an eight-angle combination lock. With a giant protractor, students measure angles and recreate them in game space, helping them to accrue first-hand experience into the nature and relationship of complementary and supplementary angles.

Evoquest (3)
This racing game promotes critical thinking, problem solving and team work while mixing physical interaction with a digital interface. Players find themselves in a tropical rainforest and must help their creature's species win a race for survival. The environment constantly changes, affecting the species' survival rate which requires the children to adapt quickly to save them.

Push (4)
This game explores the concept of work across inclined planes. Players experience mechanical work as a function of energy and distance, as they help teams of tiny creatures push objects up inclined planes of various heights and distances. The game mimics the exertion of force within a frictionless plane, giving players a real-life physical feeling for the relationship between work and energy.

(1)

(4)

(3)

(2)

Coop Himmelb(l)au
Wolf D. Prix & Partner GmbH
Pavilion 21 Mini Opera Space

Munich, Germany, *2010*

This 300 seat dismountable pavilion creates a hyper geometric space for enjoying experimental performances of the Bavarian State Opera. The light weight structure allows for the pavilion to be moved and reconstructed while keeping the acoustic integrity of the space intact. The highly angular project functions not only as an eye catching architectural specimen but also as a fine-tuned soundscape. Formally generated through the frequency analysis and parametric interpretation of the song "Purple Haze" by Jimi Hendrix and a passage from "Don Giovanni" by Mozart, the faceted geometry of this pavilion deflects noise while reflecting and absorbing sound.

Zaha Hadid Architects
Une Architecture

Paris, France, *2011*

Through the application of fluid forms, this torus-like exhibition pavilion provides differentiated and visually enticing experiences for visitors. By utilizing the existing quality of the sculpted internal walls and space divisions, the project generates rhythmical spatial sequences. A parametrically derived special structure unfolds within the pavilion to exhibit, display, and organize thematic hotspots. Media interventions such as projected animations cluster at strategic points of interest, highlighting parts of Zaha Hadid's extensive body of work through architectural models, silver paintings, and wall reliefs.

Heatherwick Studio
UK Pavilion, Seed Cathedral

Shanghai, China, *2010*

Representing the United Kingdom in the Shanghai 2010 Expo, this visually confounding pavilion produces a cutting edge exhibition space rich in atmosphere and aesthetic value. The Seed Cathedral, which stands a direct manifestation of the exhibition content, serves as a platform to showcase the work of the Royal Botanical Gardens and their Millennium Seedbank. The pavilion comprises 60,000 transparent 7.5-meter-long optical strands, each embedded with a seed at its tip. During the day, the interior illuminates only though a diffused daylight that filters past each seed and through each optical hair. At night, light sources inside each rod allow the entire structure to glow. As the wind moves past, these hairs sway gently, resulting in an impressive blurring effect that passes over the entire structure. After the Expo, the Seed Cathedral's optic hairs, each containing a huge potential of life, were distributed across hundreds of schools across both China and the UK.

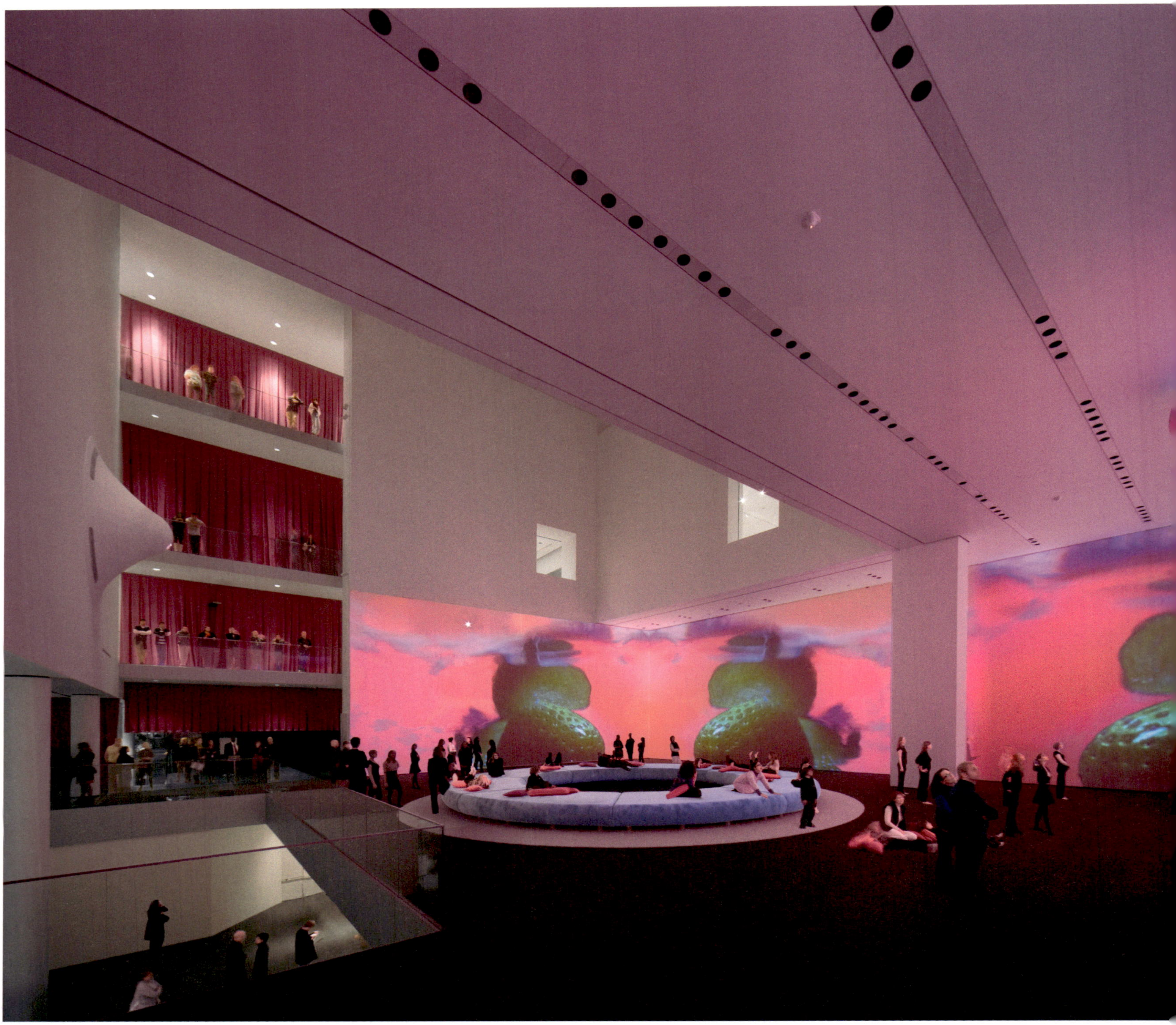

Pipilotti Rist

Pour Your Body Out (7354 Cubic Meters)

New York, USA, *2008*

This installation, located in the cavernous central atrium of the Museum of Modern Art in New York, provides a giant blue circular couch for observing an expansive video projection spanning across three walls. The film transforms the generally cold and anonymous space into an intimate theater saturated with color and a sense of community.

Tyngkraft, var min vän (Gravity Be My Friend)

Liverpool, UK / Stockholm, Sweden, *2007*

This surreal installation comprised of two biomorphic piles of carpets in the center of the space beckons visitors to lie upon them and gaze at a film of vibrant dreamlike sequences projected on the ceiling. Reorienting art from wall to ceiling creates surprising opportunities for collaboratively occupying spaces and generates new perspectives for contemplating ones surroundings.

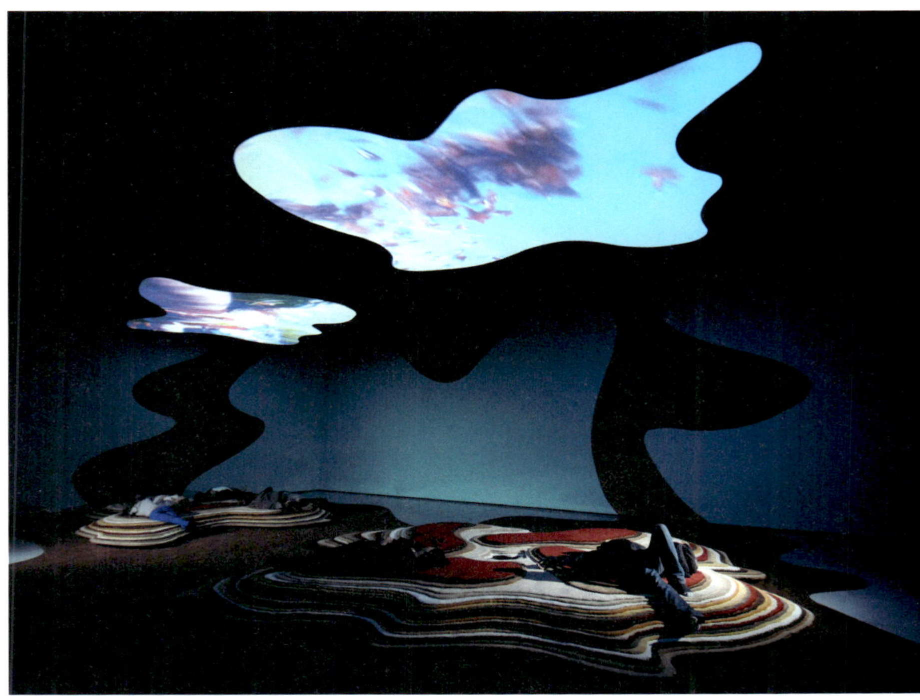

J. Mayer H. Architects
Danfoss Universe

Nordborg, Denmark, *2007*

A startling silhouette, inspired by geological formations, serves as the form of this unusual science park. The active groundscape modulates according to function and location in the surrounding complex. The endpoints of the project blur the line between interior and exterior by transforming adjacent outdoor spaces into display areas for projection surfaces related to the temporary exhibitions located inside the main building. Embedded in an agricultural landscape, this science park provides unique spaces which articulate the fusion of outdoor landscape and indoor exhibition.

Encore Heureux

Petit Bain

Paris, France, *2011*

Despite being inspired by the constraints of navigation, Petit Bain is not a boat, but in fact a building floating on the Seine. Built in a shipyard outside Paris, the project remains permanently moored at Le Port de la Gare in the heart of the city. The building comprises three levels and includes a double-height concert hall in the hull. A large, suspended buoy coated with mirror facets fills this space with glinting light. To contrast with the hull and the surrounding steel structure, pine plywood and wooden slats clad the exterior surfaces. An outdoor garden on the terrace provides an unusual exterior space that can be enjoyed by visitors and the general public along the riverfront. From shades that range from bright yellow to pale green, the hull, decks and access points playfully introduce this island in the city to the people of Paris.

MUSIC BOXES
MUSIC BOXES

BDP

Music Boxes Shipping Container Installation

Manchester, UK, *2011*

A mini city of shipping containers serves as the new home of Children's BBC in the UK. This musical playground accommodates children from six months to seven years in age. The 78 steel units stack in an irregular pattern, eschewing the traditional linear logic of containers to create an elliptical, enveloping shape reminiscent of the natural geometry and symmetry of sound.Other features evocative of shipping include a sail-like canopy, formed from wire rigging and truck tarpaulins, suspended over the central area and giant, stenciled, signage panels affixed to the ends of the containers. Capturing the spirit of the shipping container while integrating inventive spaces for play and exploration, this project offers miniature performance spaces, customized recording and animation studios, and interactive installations allowing the very young to explore a fantastical world of sound and music.

Index

BDP
United Kingdom
www.bdp.com
pp. 264-265
Music Boxes Shipping Container Installation
Client: MIF Creative, BBC, Salford City Council, Abu Dhabi Festival
Photos: Daniel Hopkinson

Benamor Duarte Architecture
Portugal
www.benamorduarte.com
pp. 156-157
Onion Pinch
with Caterina Tiazzoldi
Client: University North Carolina College of Art+Architecture / Arke Danza & Experimenta Design / Metropolitano de Lisboa
Design: Caterina Tiazzoldi, Eduardo Benamor Duarte, Team: M.Pianosi, T. Branquino, M.Fassino, L.Croce, K.Seaman
Photos: Sebastiano Pellion di Persano, Monica Pianosi, Caterina Tiazzoldi

BIG & JDS
Denmark
www.big.dk
p. 168
Maritime Youth House
Client: Kvarterløft Copenhagen, Loa Fund
Partner-In-Charge: Bjarke Ingels, Collaborator: Julien De Smedt, Projekt Architects: Henning Stüben, Annette Jensen, Team: Dorte Børresen, Finn Nørkjær, Jørn Jensen
Photos: Carsten Kring, Julien De Smedt, Mads Hilmer, Paolo Rosselli
p. 169
Sjakket Youth Centre
Client: Sjakket Youth Centre, Realdania
Partner-in-Charge: Bjarke Ingels, Collaborator: Julien De Smedt, Project Leader: Sophus Søbye, Team: Bo Benzon, Christian Dam, David Zahle, Julie Schmidt-Nielsen, Kathrin Gimmel, Louise Steffensen, Mia Frederiksen, Nanna Gyldholm Møller, Nina Ter-Borch, Ole Elkjær-Larsen, Ole Nannberg, Olmo Ahlmann, Søren Lambertsen, Narisara Ladawal
Photos: Vegar Moen

Blitz
USA
www.designblitzsf.com
pp. 214-215
Skype North American Headquarters
Client: Skype
Photos: Matthew Millman

BuroKoek
Netherlands
www.burokoek.nl
p. 204
New Office Space of Recycled Wood
Woodwork: Jolanda Slegers, Contractor: P-Kwadraat
Photos: Michel Kievits

C

C. F. Møller Architects
Denmark
www.cfmoller.com
pp. 148-149
Aarhus gymnastics and Motor Skills Hall
Client: VIK Gymnastik
Photos: Poul Nyholm, Julian Weyer
pp. 222-223
Second phase of the Darwin Centre
Client: Natural History Museum
Photos: Torben Eskerod

Carve
Netherlands
www.carve.nl
p. 132
Bijlmerpark
Carve with Marie-Laure Hoedemakers
Client: The municipality of Amsterdam
Photos: Carve
p. 133
Melis Stokepark
Client: The municipality of The Hague
Photos: Carve

Carrilho da Graça arquitectos
João Luís Carrilho da Graça
Portugal
www.jlcg.pt
pp. 56-57
Renovation and Extension of the German School of Lisbon
Photos: © FG+SG - Fotografia de Arquitectura, © João Silveira Ramos
pp. 81-83
School of Music of the Polytechnic Institute
Photos: © FG+SG - Fotografia de Arquitectura, © João Silveira Ramos

Caterina Tiazzoldi / Nuova Ordentra
Italy
www.tiazzoldi.org
p. 236
The Social Cave
with Mirko Arcese and Luca Biada
Client: Cosmit Salone Satellite – Marva Griffin
Design Team: B. Suite, D. Cashen, J. Zaratiegui, M. Fassino, V. Roether, A. Robinson, A. Shim, A. Kim, B. Brichta, C. Handal, C. Pope, D. Kaltis, E. Fammartino, E. Kapompasopoulou, E. Iannace, E. Bauer, F. Schmitt , G. Valdes, G. Lalli, H. Lee Oh, J. Choi, J. Dornic, K. Thorn, K. Lents , M. Gonzales, M. Rosso, Y. Kim, S. Ngy,
Photos: Alberto Ferrero, Ben Brichta

Cedric Bomford
with Elke Reichel Architekten
Germany
www.dorten.com
pp. 186, 202-203
Dorten office
Client: Dorten GmbH
Photos: Manuel Wagner, Frank Martin Dietrich

Coelacanth K&H Architects
Kazumi Kudo & Hiroshi Horiba
Japan
www.coelacanth-kandh.co.jp
pp. 118-119
Kanazawa Umimirai Library
Client: Kanazawa City
Photos: Satoshi Asakawa

Coop Himmelb(l)au
Wolf D. Prix & Partner ZT GmbH
Austria
www.coop-himmelblau.at
pp. 88-89
Central Los Angeles Area High School #9 for the Visual and Performing Arts
Client: LAUSD, Los Angeles Unified School District, CA, USA
Photos: Duccio Malagamba
pp. 254-255
Pavilion 21 MINI Opera Space

Cottrell & Vermeulen Architecture
United Kingdom
www.cv-arch.co.uk
pp. 44, 76-77
Krishna-Avanti Primary School
Client: The i-Foundation
Photos: Anthony Coleman

D

Dan Pearlman
Germany
danpearlman.com
p. 227
MTV Headquarters
Architect: Macus Fischer
Client: MTV Networks
Photos: diephotodesigner.de
p. 235
Elise's Island
Architect: Macus Fischer
Client: KEH
Photos: diephotodesigner.de

DAP STUDIO
Italy
www.dapstudio.com
p. 122
Elsa Morante Library
Client: Lonate Ceppino Municipality
Contributors: Alessia Mosci, Paolo Vimercati, Fabio Pelizzari, Structures: GB. Scolari, Facilities: M. Piantoni, A. Bronzoni
Photos: Luigi Filetici

Die Baupiloten
Germany
www.baupiloten.com
pp. 34-35
Kindertagesstätte Taka-Tuka-Land
Client: ASB Kinder- und Jugendhilfe gGmbH (jetzt: Orte für Kinder GmbH)
pp. 52-53
Carl-Bolle-Grundschule
Client: Jahn, Mack und Partner
pp. 54-55
Erika-Mann-Grundschule II
Client: Stattbau GmbH
Photos: Jan Bitter

Henning Larsen Architects
Denmark
www.henninglarsen.com
pp. 38-39
Elverhøj Day Care Center
Client: Municipality of Holbæk
Photos: Thorbjoern Hansen
pp. 160-161
Harpa - Reykjavik Concert Hall And Conference Centre
Client: Austurnhofn TR– East Harbour Project Ltd.
Photos: Nic Lehoux

Huma Arquitectura
Spain
www.huma.es
p. 62
Nursery – Elementary School
Client: Torre-Pacheco Town Hall
Architects: Alberto Amorós Martínez, José Amorós Martínez, Collaborator, Project manager: Eduardo José Barceló García
Photos: David Frutos

I-J

i29
Netherlands
www.i29.nl
pp. 50-51
School 01
Client: Caland Lyceum
pp. 200-201
office 03
Client: gummo
p. 201
office 04
Client: Tribal DDB

Institute of Play
USA
instituteofplay.org
pp. 252-253
SMALLab at Play
Client: Institute of Play

J. Mayer H. Architects
Germany
www.jmayerh.de
p. 262
Danfoss Universe
Client: Danfoss Universe, Denmark

K-L

Karl-Heinz Winkens & Marcel Klebs
Germany
www.winkens.de
pp. 28-29
Forscherkindergarten Apfelbäumchen

KARO*
Germany
www.karo-architekten.de
p. 124
Open-Air-Library
Client: City of Magdeburg
Photos: Anja Schlamann

KidsPatch
Serbia Montenegro
www.kids-patch.com
p. 240
KidsPatch Mini-Lab
Client: Sound & Visions Festival
KidsPatch mini-lab conducted by Nana Radenković and Lukatoyboy, Thanks to Saša Tkačenko
Photos: Luka Knežević-Strika

KIT Universität Karlsruhe Fachgebiete Tragkonstruktionen & Building Lifecycle Management
Germany
fgt.ieb.kit.edu / blm.ieb.kit.edu
p. 234
Roll-It - Guerilla Housing
Client: KIT - Karlsruher Institut für Technologie
Photos: Sebastian Salopiata

KOZ Architectes
Christophe Ouhayoun & Nicolas Ziesel
France
www.koz.fr
pp. 162-163
Le Ruban
Client: Ville de Saint Cloud
Photos: Stephen Lucas

kwint Architects
Netherlands
www.kwintarchitecten.nl
p. 107
Culture Campus Vleuterweide
Client: City of Utrecht
Photos: Stijn Poelstra

Linie Zwei
Germany
www.linie-2.de
p. 113
Robi Mobile Library
Client: City of Heilbronn
Photos: Annette Diehl Fotografie

M

Magén Arquitectos
Spain
www.magenarquitectos.com
pp. 18-19
Kindergarten Rosales del Canal
Client: Government of Aragon
Photos: Jesús Granada

Mathieu Lehanneur
France
www.mathieulehanneur.fr
pp. 154-155
Kid's Workshop
Client: Centre Pompidou
Photos: Herve Veronese, Felipe Ribon
p. 190
LaboBrain
Client: Le Laboratoire
Photos: Fabien Thouvenin

McBride Charles Ryan
Australia
www.mcbridecharlesryan.com.au
pp. 74-75
Penleigh and Essendon Grammar School – Junior Boys Building
Client: Penleigh and Essendon Grammar School
Principal Architects: Rob McBride, Debbie-Lyn Ryan, Project team: Benedikt Josef, Amelia Borg, Natasha Maben
Photos: John Gollings

MONSTRUM
Denmark
monstrum.dk
p. 144
The Sperm Whale at the North Sea Oceanarium
Client: The North Sea Oceanarium
p. 145
The Parrot
Client: Copenhagen City Council
p. 145
Rasmus Klump land
Client: TIVOLI

N-O

Nieto Sobejano Arquitectos
Fuensanta Nieto – Enrique Sobejano
Spain
www.nietosobejano.com
pp. 172-173
Interactive Museum of the History of Lugo
Client: Ayuntamiento de Lugo
Photos: Fernando Alda

NSMH - Nevzat Sayın Mimarlık Hizmetleri
pp. 176-177
Yahsibey Summer School
Client: Yahsibey Workshops
Emre Senan Institution
Photo: Cemal Emden, Nevzat Sayin, NSMH

Numen / For Use
Belgium
www.z33.be
pp. 128, 150
Net
Client: Z33 - House for contemporary art
Photos: Kristof Vrancken

O*GE Architects Merav (Salush) Eitan & Gaston Zahr
Israel
www.oge-group.com
p. 233
Giant Birdsnest for breeding new ideas
Client: O*GE Creative Group

one fine day und FH Trier
Germany
www.o-f-d.net
p. 239
Treehugger
Client: HWK Koblenz
Research-project in collaboration with our department digital design at the university of applied sciences, Trier
Team: Dipl.-Ing.(FH) Jan Busemeyer, Dipl.-Ing. (FH) Frank Stolz, Jan Weber, Gabriel Wüstner, Eva Ziegler, Peter Zock
Photos: Roland Borgmann

Supermachine Studio
Thailand
supermachine.wordpress.com
pp. 84-85
BUCC, Bangkok University Creative Center
Client: Bangkok University
Photos: Jaroonrat Vithoosuwan, Pitupong Chaowakul

SUPERPOOL
Turkey
superpool.org
p. 125
Open Library
Client: Platform Garanti
Photos: Iwan Baan

T

Taranta Creations
China
www.enrico-taranta.com
pp. 196-197
Red Town Office Space
Architects: Enrico Taranta, Juriaan Calis,Giorgio Radojkovic
Client: Taranta Creations
Photos: Shen Qiang from Shen Photo

Telekom Laboratoires
Germany
www.creation-center.de
pp. 210-211
Creation Center
Client: Telekom Laboratories
Interior Developement: Werkstatt für Unbeschaffbares
Photos: André Ludwig

Tezuka Architects
Takaharu & Yui Tezuka
Japan
www.tezuka-arch.com
pp. 40-41
Ring Around a Tree
Client: Montessori School Fuji Kindergarten
Structure Engineer: OHNO JAPAN Co., Ltd/ OHNO HIROFUMI, Lighting Designer: Masahide Kakudate/Lighting Architect&Associates
Photos: Katsuhisa Kida/FOTOTECA, Tezuka Architects
pp. 42-43
Fuji Kindergarten
Client: Montesori School Fuji Kindergarten
Creative Director: Kashiwa Sato Lighting Designer: Masahide Kakudate/Lighting Architect&Associates
Photos: Katsuhisa Kida/FOTOTECA, Tezuka Architects
pp. 151-153
Woods of Net
Client: Hakone Open-Air Museum
Architects: Takaharu+Yui Tezuka/Tezuka Architects, Norihide Imagawa(structure design)/ TIS&Partners
Artist: Toshiko Horiuchi Macadam(artwork)/ Interplay Design&Manufacturing
Photos: Katsuhisa Kida/FOTOTECA

THAM & VIDEGÅRD ARKITEKTER
Sweden
www.tvark.se
pp. 8-9
Tellus Nursery School
Client: Vasakronan
Chief architects: Bolle Tham and Martin Videgård, Project architect: Eric Engström, Collaborators: Mårten Nettelbladt, Johan Björkholm, Karolina Nyström, Marcus Andrén, Julia Schönbrunn, Andreas Helgesson
Photos: Åke E:son Lindman

THE XSS LIMITED
Catherine Cheung
Hong Kong
www.thexss.com
pp. 36-37
Starlit Learning Centre
Client: Starlit Learning Centre
Photos: Catherine Cheung, Eddie Yeung

Total Tool BA
Argentina
www.totaltool.com.ar
p. 208
Urban Station
Client: Urban Station SA
Project leaders: Darío Fischman and Juan Kayser, Lighting design: Arturo Peruzzotti, Graphics: Juan Pablo Russo, Contractor: NPC Construcciones
Photos: Sergio Esmoris

TYIN tegnestue
Norway
www.tyintegnestue.no
pp. 126-127
Safe Haven Library
Collaborator: Rintala Eggertsson Architects, built by Professors and students from the Norwegian University of Science and Technology

U-W

Uuushh – Andrea Paoletti
Italy
uuushh.com
p. 209
The Hub Rovereto
Client: The Hub Trentino
Photos: Francesco Pernigo

Van Rooijen Nourbakhsh Architecten
Netherlands
www.vanrooijenarchitecten.nl
p. 24
De Ridderhof – After School Day Care
Client: KMN Kind&Co
Photos: CornbreadWorks
p. 25
Playground building
Client: City of Utrecht
Photos: CornbreadWorks

Verstas Architects
Finland
www.verstasarchitects.com
pp. 64-65
Kirkkojärvi Comprehensive School
Client: City of Espoo
Photos: Tuomas Uusheimo

Wiel Arets Architects
Netherlands
wielaretsarchitects.nl
pp. 114-115
University Library Utrecht UBU
Client: Utrecht University
Photos: Jan Bitter

wurm + wurm architekten ingenieure gmbh
Germany
www.wurm-wurm.de
p. 112
Media Centre Oberkirch
Client: Stadt Oberkirch

Y-Z

Yoshimasa Tsutsumi
China
tsuaa.com
p. 167
Anzas Entertainment Dance Studio
Client: Anzas Entertainment
Photos: Misae Hiromatsu

Zaha Hadid Architects
United Kingdom
www.zaha-hadid.com
pp. 256-257
UNE ARCHITECTURE
Client: Institut du Monde Arabe
Design: Zaha Hadid and Patrik Schumacher, Exhibition Team: Thomas Vietzke, Manon Janssens, Woody K.T. Yao, Jens Borstelmann, Sofia Daniilidou, Torsten Broeder, Tiago Correia, Danilo Arsic, Victor Orive, Mostafa El Sayed, Christoph Wunderlich, Martin Krcha, Niki Berry, Claudia Fruianu, Daniel Widrig, Filipa Gomes, Artist Consultant: Antonio de Campos, Production: AIA Production (APC+AIA) Renaud Sabari and Alexandra
Photos: Francois Lacour, courtesy of Institut du Monde Arabe

Learn for Life
New Architecture for New Learning

Edited by Sven Ehmann, Sofia Borges, Robert Klanten
Text and preface by Sofia Borges
Layout by Birga Meyer, Matthias Hübner, Simon Becker for Gestalten
Typefaces: Malaussène by Laure Afchain, Nautinger by Moritz Esser
Foundry: www.gestaltenfonts.com
Cover by Matthias Hübner and Simon Becker for Gestalten
Cover photography (clockwise from top left):
Nacasa & Partners Inc., Emilio P. Doiztuǎ, Minoru Iwasaki,
BaO Architects, Laura Stamer, Victor Schallhauser, David Frutos, Prooff, Jan Bitter, Andreas Meichsner, Miran Kambic

Project management by Vanessa Diehl for Gestalten
Production management by Martin Bretschneider for Gestalten
Proofreading by Transparent Language Solutions
Printed by Livonia Print, Riga
Made in Europe

Published by Gestalten, Berlin 2012
ISBN 978-3-89955-414-4

For more information, please visit www.gestalten.com.

Bibliographic information published by the Deutsche Nationalbibliothek.
The Deutsche Nationalbibliothek lists this publication in the Deutsche Nationalbibliografie; detailed bibliographic data are available online at http://dnb.d-nb.de.

None of the content in this book was published in exchange for payment by commercial parties or designers; Gestalten selected all included work based solely on its artistic merit.

This book was printed on paper certified by the FSC®.

FSC www.fsc.org MIX Paper from responsible sources FSC® C002795

Gestalten is a climate-neutral company. We collaborate with the non-profit carbon offset provider myclimate (www.myclimate.org) to neutralize the company's carbon footprint produced through our worldwide business activities by investing in projects that reduce CO_2 emissions (www.gestalten.com/myclimate).

myclimate
Protect our planet